GROVE PRESS MODERN DRAMATISTS

Grove Press Modern Dramatists

Series Editors: *Bruce King* and *Adele King*

Published Titles

Further titles in preparation

GROVE PRESS MODERN DRAMATISTS

JOHN ARDEN

Frances Gray

Grove Press, Inc., New York

First published in 1982 by
THE MACMILLAN PRESS LTD.,
London and Basingstoke

First Evergreen Edition 1982
First Printing 1982
ISBN: 0–394–62415–7
Library of Congress Catalog Card Number: 82–47993

Printed in Hong Kong

GROVE PRESS INC.,
196 West Houston Street,
New York, N.Y. 10014

Contents

List of Plates

1. *Live Like Pigs*, the Royal Court, 1958: Robert Shaw as Blackmouth, Alan Dobie as Col, Frances Cuka as Daffodil. Photograph: Zoë Dominic
2. *Serjeant Musgrave's Dance*, the Royal Court, 1959: the original production directed by Lindsay Anderson. Ian Bannen played Serjeant Musgrave. Photograph: Snowdon
3. *Serjeant Musgrave's Dance*, the Royal Court, 1965: directed by Jane Howell, with Joseph Grieg as Bludgeon, Bernard Gallagher as the Pugnacious Collier, Sebastian Shaw as Private Attercliffe and Victor Henry as Private Sparky. Photograph: Zoë Dominic
4. *The Hero Rises Up*, original production by John Arden and Margaretta d'Arcy, the Roundhouse, 1968: Henry Woolf as Nelson, Bettina Jonic as Lady Hamilton. Photograph: Donald Cooper
5. *The Island of the Mighty*, the Aldwych, 1972: Patrick Allen as Arthur. Photograph: Donald Cooper

Acknowledgements

The author wishes to thank the University of Sheffield for leave of absence and a grant to write this book; John Arden, Margaretta D'Arcy, Alfred Bradley, Mike Dyer, Phil Roberts; the archives of the Royal Court, the National Theatre, and the Senate House; the British Institute of Recorded Sound; the students of Sheffield University who took part in *Ars Longa, Vita Brevis*. Special thanks are due to Jay Woolrich for preparing the index.

For my father

Editors' Preface

The *Grove Press Modern Dramatists* is an international series of introductions to major and significant nineteenth- and twentieth-century dramatists, movements and new forms of drama in Europe, Great Britain, America and new nations such as Nigeria and Trinidad. Besides new studies of great and influential dramatists of the past, the series includes volumes on contemporary authors, recent trends in the theatre and on many dramatists, such as writers of farce, who have created theatre 'classics' while being neglected by literary criticism. The volumes in the series devoted to individual dramatists include a biography, a survey of the plays, and detailed analysis of the most significant plays, along with discussion, where relevant, of the political, social, historical and theatrical context. The authors of the volumes, who are involved with theatre as playwrights, directors, actors, teachers and critics, are concerned with the plays as theatre and discuss such matters as performance, character interpretation and staging, along with themes and contexts.

Grove Press Modern Dramatists are written for people

interested in modern theatre who prefer concise, intelligent studies of drama and dramatists, without jargon and an excess of footnotes.

BRUCE KING
ADELE KING

1
Introduction

Between 1956 and 1961, the Royal Court Theatre made about £50,000 producing the plays of John Osborne and lost £14,857 producing those of John Arden. Both dramatists received notices which ranged from the vituperative to the lyrical. Both won *Evening Standard* awards for the most promising playwright of the year, Osborne for *Look Back in Anger* in 1956 and Arden for *Serjeant Musgrave's Dance* in 1959, an award he shared with Arnold Wesker whose play *Roots* was also produced at the Royal Court. Both were widely regarded as major figures in the so-called New Wave of British dramatists that changed the face of the English theatre in the mid-1950s. It is not the intention of this book to examine the financial side of Arden's work; but to look at those two sums of money is to learn a good deal about the theatrical context in which his early work was set.

It is appropriate to begin an account of the British theatre of the 50s by talking about money, because for half the decade money seemed to be its chief preoccupation.

Shows like *Salad Days*, *The Boy Friend*, *The Reluctant Debutante* and *Wild Thyme* were geared rather to providing the public with a good night out for which they were happy to pay, than to emotional or intellectual excitement. Rattigan, Coward and Priestley all had plays running in the West End, well-carpentered pieces that kept their creators a long way above the breadline. Money was also much in evidence within the plays themselves, dealing as they largely did with the fortunes of the upper to upper-middle classes. As Kenneth Tynan sourly remarked, 'To become eligible for detailed dramatic treatment, it was usually necessary either to have an annual income of more than three thousand pounds or to be murdered in the house of someone who did.'[1]

Tynan was not alone in bewailing the intellectual and linguistic poverty of British theatre. Critics spoke hopefully of John Whiting and Graham Greene, wondered if T. S. Eliot and Christopher Fry were going to usher in a new age of verse drama (they did not) and looked to Europe for a more vigorous theatrical life. When the English Stage Company, led by George Devine, leased the Royal Court Theatre with the avowed intention of establishing a 'writer's theatre', where new work could be given a sympathetic hearing and where commercial interests would not be paramount, it was making a brave gesture of faith. The gesture paid off; most of the major British dramatists of the next few years were to have work presented at and encouraged by the Court (indeed, they still do) until, despite the powerful presence of other bravely experimental managements such as that at Stratford East, it became almost synonymous with the so-called Renaissance in British drama. The Court was, as the box-office receipts for Arden's plays make clear, sometimes an expensive Renaissance.

That the play which really caught the public imagination and, after a shaky start, saved the Court's finances, was *Look Back in Anger* shows the conservatism of taste among the theatre-going public, even at this most progressive of theatres. *Look Back in Anger* was revolutionary only in content, not in form. Its hero was exciting, its language passionate and vigorous. It articulated the response of the educated young towards the collapse of the British Empire (this was the era of Cyprus, Suez and the Mau Mau) and the changes in sexual and social standards, whereas many of its contemporaries languished in some pre-war cloud-cuckooland where conflict was reduced to a tennis match offstage. But at the same time, it failed to challenge the accepted idea of what theatre really *is*; it could be discussed using the same vocabulary as the latest offering by Terence Rattigan or William Douglas-Home. Controversy raged around the central figure, Jimmy Porter; but, like him or loathe him, call him an 'anti-hero' (a popular term of the decade), or, as Somerset Maugham did, 'scum', nobody was in any doubt as to the sort of play he featured in. Even *Woman's Own* carried an article about it, sitting cosily beside a recipe for 'sweetheart cake'. Disturbing the play might be, but it was also thoroughly accessible, the perfect play to discuss at parties; this, as much as its undoubted merits, was a major reason for its financial success.

Its fame also suggests the reason for Arden's lack of it. To watch a play by Arden, or to participate in one, is to engage in a debate about theatre – what it is for, and whom it is for. It is a debate which Arden and, latterly, his co-writer Margaretta D'Arcy, have continued to develop, and into which they have drawn many people from walks of life far removed from the West End – trades unionists, Girl Guides, the parishioners of their local church. Their relationship with the critics is often stormy; ironically, Arden's current work is often compared unfavourably with early 'masterpieces' like *Serjeant Musgrave's Dance*. But to go back and look at those early reviews of this 'masterpiece' is to see at once how reluctant both public and critics then were to join the debate at all. The notices are not only, on the whole, disparaging, they are also very uncertain about the nature of the plays. The word 'pretentious' appears more than once. At the time the word was virtually synonymous with 'experimental' and, in a climate in which T. S. Eliot took pains to select titles like *The Cocktail Party* for his plays to prove that they were not highbrow, 'pretentious' denoted an eighth deadly sin. Harold Hobson described *Serjeant Musgrave's Dance* as:

> another frightful ordeal. It is time someone reminded our advanced dramatists that the principal function of the theatre is to give pleasure. It is not the principal function of the theatre to strengthen peace, to improve morality or to establish a good social system. Churches, international associations and political parties already exist for those purposes. It is the duty of the theatre, not to make men better, but to render them harmlessly happy.[2]

The *Manchester Evening News* concurred, with the by-line WAR PLAY IS DULL SERMON. *Punch* also used the word 'sermon' and took particular exception to the songs: 'When Mr. Arden can think of no better employment for his characters he lets them sing the tag-ends of doggerel ballads', it complained, concluding the review with the choice epithet 'lump of absurdity'.[3] To call a play a lump or a sermon or an ordeal is tantamount to denying that it is

4

a play; and this in turn implies a strong preconception of what a play really is. It is interesting that some of the more favourable reviews of *Serjeant Musgrave's Dance* – notably that of Alan Brien in the *Spectator* – looked to Europe when making comparisons. Brien referred to Ibsen and Brecht, both of whom had initiated debates as to the nature of theatre through their plays. It is greatly to the credit of the Royal Court that its continuing support in the face of empty seats – George Devine even put out a pamphlet in which Osborne, Wesker and N. F. Simpson declared their belief in the quality of Arden's work – allowed Arden to initiate his own debate in England.

It is necessary to look a little more closely at the theatrical tradition that Arden and others were beginning to challenge, for it is still very much with us; in fact, thanks to television, it is the tradition with which most of us grow up and which still shapes the preconceptions of most people when they enter a theatre. This is the concept of the stage as magic box, a room with one wall removed allowing us to look in and see people apparently behaving as they do in real life; they hold conversations which sound like everyday speech – although you only have to place the text of a play alongside a taped conversation to realize that this is a carefully structured fiction. The things that happen on stage might happen in real life – although, again, closer examination reveals that real life is both more tedious and more bizarre than the meticulously patterned happenings in the magic box. This tradition is grounded in the work done by Stanislavski in the Russian theatre at the end of the last century and the beginning of this one. Its keynote might be described as 'emotional truth'. The actor must convince us by the way he behaves that he is inhabiting a real world just like our own, and in order to stress the autonomy of his world must ignore ours completely. In *Building a Character* Stanislavski writes in the persona of a young student learning to present a character of his own imagining:

As soon as I was in this other man's skin my attitude towards you underwent a radical change. I even had the sensation that I was not conversing with you but with someone entirely different . . . in that other person's skin I went as far as I liked. . . . 'Yes, but what did you feel when faced with the black hole of the proscenium arch?', asked one of the other students. 'I never even noticed it. I was so taken up with something far more interesting which absorbed my whole being.'[4]

The Stanislavskian actor commits himself to the reality of the part by denying the reality of the audience; we are only a 'black hole' which he will, with luck, forget altogether. Stanislavski was adamant that the actor can 'achieve this fusion of himself and the character he is representing only if he learns to love him.'[5] If the actor is a good one, this love will transmit itself to us; the actor will show us the character as he appears to himself, he will teach us to view the world from the character's point of view. We will understand and forgive faults; we will become aware of the human traits we have in common and in all probability identify strongly with the feelings and actions of the character.

The pull of the magic box is powerful, as the viewing figures for family-life soap operas on television will confirm; most of us feel competent to judge a play conceived in these terms; we will talk of actors as 'convincing' or 'out of character', since we feel we know their characters well enough to make this sort of judgement. At best, this form of theatre can be of very high quality indeed; but when this is the case, as with the plays of Chekhov, there is also a sense of tension, that the form is not totally adequate to what is being said. Raymond Williams has described it thus:

> In Chekhov or Ibsen . . . what is visible and directly expressible is no more than a counterpoint to the unrealised life – the inner and common desires, fears, possibilities – which struggles to find itself in just this solidly staged world. When we speak of naturalism, we must distinguish between this passion for the whole truth, for the liberation of what can not yet be said or done, and the confident and even complacent representation of things as they are, that things are what they seem.[6]

On the whole, however, the naturalistic theatre is so seductive that we accept its conventions without thinking and it rarely occurs to us to think seriously about it as a form to which there are alternatives. Our blindness is reinforced by scholarship at every level from the junior school onwards. There can be few readers of this book who did not spend a good deal of homework time on questions which began 'Give a short character study of the following'.

The theatre for which Arden had begun to write was, however, beginning to struggle slowly and painfully with alternative forms, with the fact that 'If art reflects life, it does so with special mirrors'.[7] The author of that statement, Bertolt Brecht, was only just beginning to penetrate the consciousness of British theatre practitioners, although his theories had been current in Europe since the 1920s. The indispensable Royal Court

7

lost heavily on its production of the Brecht classic *The Good Woman of Setzuan* in 1956. Some of the blame may be ascribed to the climate of hostility to all things Marxist which had been generated by the Soviet reaction to the Hungarian revolution; some, however, arose from the rather uncertain treatment of the play by a company unfamiliar with a totally different approach to theatre from the one they were used to; and some from the refusal of the audience to abandon its own preconceptions about what a play should be and do. The attempt to come to terms with the work of Brecht had, however, begun; many new dramatists of the period were to see the season of plays at the Palace Theatre (also in 1956) performed by the company Brecht himself had founded, the Berliner Ensemble, as a watershed in their writing lives. Arden was enormously impressed and later cited one of the plays performed, *Mother Courage*, as the twentieth-century play he would most like to have written. Although they differ in many significant ways, some understanding of Brecht is useful for the study of Arden; as it provides a vocabulary for the discussion of his work, something sadly lacking in the early reviews of it. What follows is of necessity the briefest of surveys.

Brecht's objection to the theatrical tradition of Stanislavski was based on the fact that, by merely describing the world, even as accurately as possible, it was tacitly recognizing, even supporting, the established order. The spectator, absorbed in the passion of another, says to himself, 'Yes, I have felt that. That's the way I am. That's only natural. . . . That's great art; everything is self-evident.'[8] Brecht wanted the theatre to be not a reflection of society but an instrument for changing it. His ideal spectator would say, 'I hadn't thought of that. That's not the way it should be. That's very strange . . . , almost unbelievable. That must stop! The sufferings of that man affect me deeply, because there is a way out for him. This is great art – nothing is self-evident.'[9]

The world shown in a Brecht play bears the stamp of its own capacity to be changed; the better world that can be made by the audience is always kept before our inner eye. To achieve this, Brecht jettisoned the stylistic virtues of the naturalistic stage – credibility, order, a coherent sequence of events. He never allowed his audience to forget that they were in a theatre. Stage and lighting effects were always clearly visible, the structure of the plays was episodic, so that the audience would attend to the point made by each scene individually rather than watching the slow development of character or situation; they did not ask 'What comes next?' because they were told, by placarded announcements or by songs. Actors did not try to convince anyone that they were the characters they played, instead they *represented* them, and spoke the lines in a way which often suggested that they were critical of their actions; there were songs which provided a commentary on the events of the play. Brecht wanted his audience as awake and alert as spectators at a boxing match, a circus, or a debate – not absorbed in the fortunes of a suffering protagonist, but critical and alive to the wider issues at stake.

The Alienation effect, as Brecht called this method of distancing the spectator from the action, has suffered from endless misinterpretation. By rejecting the idea of empathy with the tragic hero, and the idea that a play should leave the audience 'purged' of all emotion and therefore content with the world as it is, he hoped not to banish passion from the theatre but to excite different and more constructive ones – the righteous anger of the oppressed, the urgency of the sense of justice; the sheer intellectual pleasure in suddenly understanding some of the workings of society. Brecht saw man not as lone hero, but as the product of social forces which he could learn to control and change. But in the British theatre of the 1950s Brecht was regarded with a kind of patronizing suspicion; his name conjured up visions of an earnest Teutonic heaviness, despite his writings about theatre placing great stress on *Spass* – fun. And although many writers were affected by the superficial aspects of his method of presentation, they ignored the political significance of his work; he meant primarily, to them, relief from the tyranny of naturalism. Robert Bolt, for example, made use of a chorus-figure, the Common Man, in his play *A Man for all Seasons*, but his central character, Thomas More, was still the tragic hero for whose dilemma we felt empathy. Osborne made some experiments in *Luther*, both with the set and a Knight who acted as commentator, but he was still chiefly preoccupied with the feelings of one man rather than with his impact upon world thinking. The playwright of the New Wave who dealt most explicitly with politics, Arnold Wesker, made some successful inroads into non-naturalistic territory, but his best known trilogy was praised above all for its truth to the rhythms of everyday speech and action.

The cautiousness with which the British theatre approached Brecht is ironic; there is little in his work that would have surprised Ben Jonson, who used song, verse and self-conscious theatricality in comedies charged with moral passion; and the techniques of alienation Brecht used were the staple tricks of the music hall and the stand-up comic in Britain as in Germany. While audiences shied at devices aimed at reminding them that they were watching a play, not real life, no-one found it odd that the Goons, on radio, relentlessly sent up their medium instead of creating believable characters: 'I'd like to see them try this on television', grunted Neddy Seagoon of some particularly impossible feat, and audiences laughed rather than worried about the theory behind it. Arden described a vivid instance of the Alienation effect that had appealed to him in a Dublin pantomime:

> an individual dressed as a gorilla bounded onto the stage and did a lot of knockabout with two comedians, and then came leaping off into the audience . . . plonked himself down into a fat woman's lap and took her hat off, deposited her hat on a bald man, then flung its arms round another bald man and nuzzled him in the face . . . and just as you were beginning to wonder how far it was going to go the gorilla suddenly bounded back onto the stage, unzipped the costume, and it was an attractive chorus girl in a little dress. And then everybody cheered and clapped.[10]

Arden regards his own theories of theatre as derived as much from British traditions as from Brecht; it is perhaps sad that this most British of dramatists has often been made by his critics to seem alien, experimental and cold. While his reputation grew quickly, it was always couched in rather forbidding terms as critics acknowledged his power but aloofly rejected the actual plays. 'Through the haze of words I glimpse a high promise',[11] said the *Daily Mail* of his first play, *The Waters of Babylon*, and the *Liverpool Post* hailed his 'considerable talent' in *Live Like Pigs* while nominating the play 'my most sordid evening in the theatre'.[12] This paradoxical and rather begrudging attitude brought Arden an *Evening Standard* award along with the comment by one of the judges, Milton Shulman, 'I feel that he will turn up with a better play next year' – the play in question being *Serjeant Musgrave's Dance*.

To look in detail at a particular instance of a common critical response to Arden may help to underline the ambivalence with which his work is still regarded. Ronald Hayman, who has written a short book on Arden and several books on the British theatre of the last thirty years, comments of the scene in *Serjeant Musgrave's Dance* in which the barmaid Annie offers herself in turn to each of the three soldiers sleeping in the stable of the inn:

> The simple poetic images contribute to the vigour and the appeal of the writing, but, like the movement of the scene from one refusal to the next, the movement of the dialogue would be more acceptable in a ballad. Arden's indictment of military butchery depends on characterising the serjeant and his men as caught in an uncomfortable tension between morbid guilt and repentant evangelism, but it is very hard to believe that three hardened sex-starved soldiers would each reject a willing girl.[13]

This is not untypical criticism of Arden in that it isolates the source of his writing strength and assumes that it is actually a weakness, while condemning him for his failure to do things which he did not set out to do. Hayman has approached this play, and this scene, with certain preconceptions. He expects to see characters behave 'consistently'. He assumes that a play about a man like the austere Musgrave and his violent attempt to teach people the awful realities of war must centre upon the conflicts in his character and those of his associates; that the most important aspect of the play is the 'tension' between two emotional states, battling it out in front of us. He expects the actors to play the soldiers as rounded characters with past lives which we can discern from their present behaviour – here, for instance, he seems to expect them to indicate that they are 'sex-starved' and then to relieve the strain on our credulity by explaining in psychologically convincing terms why they refuse to sleep with Annie.

[A handwritten note is affixed over part of the page, reading:]

Argument w. Hayman — "expects to see characters behave consistently"

This seems to be a very clichéd assumption about soldiers and sex; ... also a dangerous assumption in that it ... what actually *happens* ... the scene. Arden/the Brecht... interested in making us question ... everyday ... individual ... s, a whole ... denotes ... e soldiers ... e in their ... We know ... eirs is no ... o preach ... war. We know that whore... is intimately connected with war – she had a lover ... nt for a soldier ... and has since become a whore to the soldiers – it's a class by itself.

In this scene, whore and soldiers interact in unexpected ways. She offers more than a simple transaction; her loving is based as much upon the idea of safety as of carnality, and it is also a fierce and conscious opposition to the hardness of 'duty' and Serjeant Musgrave, although she does not yet know the full extent of his message. The idea of 'duty', of the 'word' they have brought to the town, broods over the soldiers and their response to her; in each case they reject Annie because of the 'word'. To Hurst, the angry soldier, the 'word' of Musgrave is so strong that it cancels out desire; Attercliffe, the grey-haired soldier, sends her away with gentle but bitter words about the blood on his hands; Sparky, the young soldier who is afraid, tries to run away with her instead of settling for immediate comfort.

In this scene, then, we are chiefly aware of a force which is more powerful than everyday desires and which elicits sharply differing responses. It builds up suspense – what is going to happen at the recruiters' meeting? – but it also begins to crystallize certain attitudes to war. When Musgrave finally presents his implacable logic to the town, demanding yet more lives to pay for the senseless killing abroad, our own responses will have been partly shaped by this scene.

These responses do not depend merely on our feelings about individual characters. Arden suggested that 'a study of the roles of the women, and of Private Attercliffe, should be sufficient to remove any doubts as to where the "moral" of the play lies'. The word 'role' rather than 'character' is significant. We should be looking at the whole situation and the function of the actors within it, not speculating about whether or not we like Annie or sympathize with Attercliffe, or whether they would behave differently in another sexual context. The ballad-like structure helps us to focus on that whole; we are familiar in folk song with the triad – three wishes, three questions, three tries before you succeed – so it is not surprising that Annie goes to three men in turn, nor that the last man, Sparky, ends the episode with a violent shift in the action; his attempt to run away with Annie leads to his death. This gives the episode a satisfying shape which helps us to assess it clearly; it forms part of a long and complex sequence of events which, besides the killing of Sparky, includes the miners' attempt to steal the soldiers' Gatling and the start of riots in the town, and given a naturalistic treatment it might well have seemed shapeless and insignificant. As it is, the familiar structure compels our attention and clarifies our thinking; it does exactly what it is designed to do. Hayman, however, seems to be taking it for granted that a ballad structure would be out of place, that Arden should take pains to hide its artificiality instead of using it to serve the play.

Hayman's kind of critical attitude has bedevilled much of Arden's work. Arden's special qualities are acknowledged but the tacit assumption that he is somehow betraying the *real* cause – naturalism – is always there. In a pamphlet written for English Advanced level school candidates on *Serjeant Musgrave's Dance* (now, ironically enough, canonized as a set text) the author offers many pertinent criticisms and insights, but still finds it necessary to give 'character studies' of every figure in the play from Musgrave himself down to the Dragoon who speaks about ten lines in the penultimate scene, most of them purely functional ones like 'You're under arrest.'

The elevation of *Serjeant Musgrave's Dance* to set-book heights, however, does indicate that many of Arden's original points in the theatre debate have now been widely accepted. But the debate goes on in different areas. Arden is now attacked chiefly for the matter rather than the manner of his plays; throughout the 70s he has been moving towards a clearly defined political position and his newer work, whether written in collaboration with Margaretta D'Arcy or alone, expresses this position. The widespread critical dismay this has caused has a slightly farcical air, since many of the attacks begin by paying tribute to the early plays that were so relentlessly derogated in the 50s. Harold Hobson, for example, who some time after his vehement assault upon *Serjeant Musgrave's Dance* wrote a splendid and spirited retraction in its praise, revived his 'frightful ordeal' label when confronted with *The Island of the Mighty* in 1972. Hayman, in a recent survey of British theatre, brackets Arden with Edward Bond and John McGrath in a chapter called 'The Politics of Hatred', accusing them all of having 'sacrificed artistry to activism'.[14] In a radio broadcast in 1980 Hayman cited a statement by Trevor Griffiths that he would give up writing if he could more usefully bring about social change in other ways, and added 'Arden hasn't given up writing plays. He's just given up writing good ones'.[15]

In the following chapter I will examine in detail Arden's debate with his public about the manner and the matter of theatre, both in his own plays and in his writings about drama and politics. First, however, I will outline in more general terms his special qualities and resources as a playwright, the features which make an Arden play uniquely exciting.

2
Resources

John paddles up and down the long brown street
On two brown boats which are his two flat feet
And London houses blink at him and whisper . . . .
                                    (John Arden, *Here I come.*)

Introducing his book of essays *To Present the Pretence*,
John Arden describes some of the convictions he and
Margaretta D'Arcy share about theatre and provides a
helpful illustration: Pieter Bruegel's painting *The Battle
Between Carnival and Lent*. Its colourful and complex
energies do more than display the specific features Arden
points out; they also aptly symbolize his work as a whole.

As Arden says, the painting, despite the accuracy of its
observation, is essentially emblematic rather than
naturalistic. Everyone in it is *playing a part*; it shows a
whole village turning out to watch the figures of Carnival
and Lent fight their mock battle with a shovel and a spit.
They are plainly other villagers dressed up for the

17

occasion; their fellows take the side of Carnival or Lent by what they choose to do – they go to church, or get drunk, make love, or play guitars; they are dramatizing the conflict 'to themselves and for themselves'.[1] The whole canvas is full of people performing. In the church the priest hears confessions and acts the part of God by releasing penitents from sin; a group of actors perform the old play *The Dirty Bride*; in another corner is a man in the costume of a Wild Man or Woodwose, the feral man cut off from God and from society. As Arden points out, the central conflict between Carnival and Lent is geometrically balanced between priest and Woodwose, the force of order and the force of anarchy. Society can go on without the Wild Man, but his presence is crucial in the theatre. In a sense, despite his obscure position in the picture, he is making it all happen.

The picture presents not just a series of acts of theatre, but a *kind* of theatre, one which is clearly traceable in Arden's own plays. In the first place, it is a theatre in which the actor–audience relationship is not an active-passive one. The audience is participating fully; they are responsible for the whole spectacle and the central figures of Carnival and Lent have been chosen from among them. The show is part of their lives, part of the seasonal ritual which involves all of them: it expresses the whole of their lives, the energy of celebration and the sombreness of ·Lent, the corpse by the church and the drunken revellers making love; and to do so it uses old stories and traditions, those of the Gospel and the folk-tale. Bruegel's theatre is a social one, not a private entertainment; it is there for society – although the presence of the Wild Man also implies a force which is outside the social order, but which, through theatre, shapes and changes it.

A writer's first resource is personal experience. It is not

surprising to find that Arden's background differs markedly from those of his contemporaries of the New Wave. Osborne, Wesker and Pinter all made very direct use of their own experience. Pinter and Osborne were both actors, and their plays fitted quite comfortably into the commonly accepted theatrical structures; they work well behind the proscenium arch; although Osborne complained at its limitations, even *Luther* and *The Entertainer* do not really seem out of place there. The relationship between actor and audience is, despite the occasional use of direct address by Osborne, not very different from that in the plays which he had performed in himself. All three writers drew on events in their own lives; Pinter ascribes the sense of menace in his early work to his remembered childhood as a Jew in wartime London; Osborne's heroes are often actors, writers or at least self-dramatizers; Wesker shows on stage the Air Force barracks and the kitchen in which he had worked himself.

Arden, born in Barnsley in 1930, went to a public school in the north, Sedbergh. His early experience of theatre was limited to occasional visits to local reps and to school plays – he once played Hamlet – and his schoolboy attempts at writing did not conform to current theatrical practice but expressed things that had had an impact on his imagination in theatrical forms he had learned about from books; he recalls a piece about the Crusades and a play about the death of Hitler in the style of *Sweeney Agonistes*; and he developed an interest in the King Arthur legend that led him to make several attempts at dramatizing the subject before it found its final expression in *The Island of the Mighty*. In other words, his concept of theatre drew upon less naturalistic traditions than those predominating in the 40s and 50s; he was committed to 'artificiality' and to verse as well as prose as soon as he began to write. At university

19

– he read architecture at Cambridge and Edinburgh – he continued in the same direction. The first play of his to be performed, *All Fall Down*, was staged by the College of Art theatre group in Edinburgh and was based on images from the old-fashioned toy theatre with its crude colour and glitter and strained heroic poses. Arden says of it, 'if someone were to turn up the MS of this play and present it somewhere today, I would no doubt be embarrassed by its technical ineptitude, but I would not disown its fundamental conception.'[2]

On leaving university Arden worked in an architect's office in London, for a qualifying year followed by another as a fully fledged architect. It provided him with some material he used in his television play *Wet Fish* and, more lastingly, with a sense of structure and an awareness of the needs of the stage designer; he makes detailed and sometimes unusual demands in terms of stage shape and design. The plays he wrote at this time were of a piece with *All Fall Down* in their conscious artifice and experiment. His radio play, *The Life of Man*, used a richly textured language and jumped about in time and space to present a sea story with overtones of *The Ancient Mariner*, a magical piece with mermaids and an enigmatic Welsh shepherd who sings as he is hanged from the yard-arm. Awarded a prize on the BBC Northern Network, it drew the attention of George Devine, who later accepted *The Waters of Babylon* for a Sunday night performance-without-decor at the Royal Court. Arden became a member of the Writers' Group at the Court, which began as a discussion group for playwrights linked to the theatre but developed into a series of practical explorations of the nature of theatre under William Gaskill and Keith Johnstone. Participants included Edward Bond, David Cregan and Ann Jellicoe. Arden derived especial benefit from Devine's work with masks, which have featured in several of his plays since *The Happy Haven*. He also spoke warmly of the arrangement at the Court which allowed writers to watch rehearsals of any play they liked.

His entry into the theatre was thus very much that of a *writer* rather than an actor or director who also happened to write, and a writer whose convictions had been shaped by traditions other than those of the West End. To some extent he found acceptance on his own terms; there was always support for the experimental side of his work at the Court and the grudging appreciation of the critics did eventually materialize. But Arden also entered the theatre looking for a quality of involvement unlike that experienced by most of his contemporaries. While the Court group provided support, it was support in a situation geared to the *eventual* creation of plays. Arden wanted a real change in the relationship between actor, writer and audience, to use the audience as a resource in his work rather than the passive receptor of it. He discusses this in his preface to *Plays One:*

> I was never able to feel that I belonged in the modern theatre. I had some of the best actors and actresses in the country on my cast-lists, and I never got to know any of them much better than if I had been a member of their audiences. The audiences themselves came and went and applauded politely enough, but the distance between them in their seats and the play on the stage seemed irreducible . . . I was troubled by a general lack of warmth, a withdrawn coldness, a too-precisely-defined correctitude of artistic technique which seemed to tell the audience 'Thus far and no further – we are the professionals – actors, director, designer, author – and you are to contemplate the work we choose to show you

– if you take it in the right spirit you will probably be the better for it.' (To which the audiences naturally responded with a mute defiance and an obvious reluctance to be impressed.) When I was actually writing my scripts I had no such attitude of mind. I regarded myself as preparing a story which would be told to the audience on my behalf by the actors, which would in fact be me saying something of interest to a whole crowd of people whom I would have liked to believe my friends.[3]

While Arden continued to write for the established, professional and generally London-based theatre for some time, he also began to make experiments in what might be called community theatre, which involved actors, writers and audience in rather different ways. In these he started to write in partnership with his wife, Margaretta D'Arcy; he had already made use of her experience as an actress, creating parts which she played in his early work – she was the original Rosie in *Live Like Pigs*, and Teresa in *The Waters of Babylon*. She contributed extensively to *The Happy Haven*, written during Arden's fellowship in creative writing at Bristol University. (Arden spoke of the Bristol audiences in favourable contrast to those in London, comparing their determination to have a good time with the 'casual boredom' of those in London, and suggested that the London atmosphere might generate a bad press for plays which, in the provinces, might be seen by a fresh and unjaded eye.) Their subsequent work together pushed out new frontiers. They staged a nativity play, *The Business of Good Government*, at the Church of St Michael, Brent Knoll in Somerset, at the request of the vicar, directing it themselves with a cast of village people with little acting experience.

In 1963, when they moved to Kirbymoorside in Yorkshire, Margaretta D'Arcy began to make a film about the town and this evolved into a month-long festival, which was advertised in *Encore* thus:

> John Arden has conceived the idea of establishing a free Public Entertainment in his house. . . . No specific form of entertainment is at present envisaged but it is hoped that in the course of it the forces of Anarchy, Excitement and Expressive Energy latent in the most apparently sad person shall be given release.[4]

The festival consisted of films, Hollywood and homemade, plays, songs, fire-eating and a performance by local Guides of Arden and D'Arcy's play *Ars Longa, Vita Brevis* – in short, anything that the participants were willing to do to keep the thing going. It taught the community something about its ability to generate its own entertainment, and it taught Arden, as he wrote later in *Encore*, about the need for some sort of overall direction which could impose upon the group occasional 'neo-Stalinist purges to keep them going'[5] without taking over completely and destroying all spontaneity. Other festivals followed, in Dublin and at Beaford in Devon (not organized by Arden or D'Arcy) where they staged their play for children, *The Royal Pardon*, with local performers and resources. Arden himself played the self-righteous Constable, a character who parodies the less receptive responses to events like Kirbymoorside.

His involvement in the process of creating drama with and for particular communities took another step forward in 1967 when he worked for a few months at the Theatre Department of New York University. The original brief was simply to lecture, but he agreed to work on practical

23

projects if D'Arcy, more experienced in the field, could be formally associated with him. The students suggested putting into practice an idea he had thrown out in his preface to *The Workhouse Donkey* for an all-day performance in which the audience could wander in and out as they liked; they also wanted to examine the Vietnam war, a matter which affected them all profoundly and to which many of them might eventually be drafted. The result was a 'Carnival of War', involving not only students but fringe groups like the Bread and Puppet Theatre, who were to give important assistance later in staging *The Non-Stop Connolly Show.* Games and performances by these groups punctuated a kind of comic-strip serial by Arden and D'Arcy. The evening concluded with a kind of 'happening' engineered by Arden himself, in which he stepped into a wildly excited group to declare himself a CIA *agent provocateur* and followed this by a quiet act of civil disobedience – stepping on the American flag.

D'Arcy rather than Arden was the moving force behind the Carnival and he seemed to regard it as a learning experience for himself rather than an event for which he took chief responsibility. The value of it resided, for him, less in the political content than in the breaking down of barriers between actor and audience, creator and participant. He pointed out that, despite the immense range of possibilities for new subject matter opened up since the abolition of censorship and the taboo-breaking of the New Wave, the theatrical context in which new plays took place was not very different from that familiar to Shaw and Granville Barker, whose work appeared at the Court before it received the 'Royal' soubriquet. It did not occur to him at the time that this was a political as well as an aesthetic issue.

In 1968, Arden and D'Arcy worked for the first time

with an overtly socialist group, CAST, on their play *Harold Muggins is a Martyr*. They also ran into difficulties with the Institute of Contemporary Arts (ICA) over their Nelson play *The Hero Rises Up* and staged free performances at the Round House. In 1969 they went to India, and their experiences there brought about profound changes in the way they saw both politics and theatre. They came into contact with revolutionary groups who, for the first time, were making contact with the very bottom elements of the caste system; they observed for the first time what poverty really is. Arden described, in an interview with Pam Gems[6], the occasion when he and D'Arcy got lost after a trip round a 'model' factory and found themselves on the edge of a swamp in which naked, filthy, starving people staggered about under the weight of huge loads; he records a sudden, strong awareness that to people in this plight, all Westerners must of necessity seem like rich capitalists. They found themselves in jail over a rubber-stamp technicality, and Arden was also accused of possessing 'subversive books', which he says brought home to him the very real power of literature in a way which Europeans seldom experience. Their contact with the plays and dances of India also bore fruit in *The Island of the Mighty*.

Arden has, since the Indian visit, concentrated increasingly on community theatre, and community theatre of a political nature. Now living for most of the time in the Republic of Ireland, he has collaborated with D'Arcy on several plays dealing with Irish politics. He has participated in street theatre on local issues – D'Arcy was largely instrumental in setting up the Galway Theatre Workshop which provided instant graphic and imaginative responses to specific political issues. With D'Arcy he wrote a play about the absentee landlord problem in the local

25

community, *The Ballygombeen Bequest*, which was staged in the Falls Road as well as in England and Scotland. Arden and D'Arcy have also staged a massive theatrical project about the great crossroads in Irish history, *The Non-Stop Connolly Show*, an event almost unprecedented in the sheer scale both of its length and the number of different groups involved in its production. Arden now regards himself as a politically committed writer; this has led him, partly from choice, to devote his time to groups outside what one of his critics rather arrogantly called 'major theatres'. There *is* a sharp division in his work – the Indian experience can be taken as the boundary – but most of his current activities can be seen as logical steps in the debate he initiated in 1957, and the resources he brings to bear upon them are fundamentally the same.

The most immediately striking feature of his plays is their use of words; it is sometimes possible to miss or misinterpret other aspects of his style, but it is apparent to the most casual eye or ear that he is using words in a way quite unlike any of his contemporaries. This is most obvious when he is writing verse, but the quality of his prose also sets him apart. His first play to be performed at the Royal Court, *The Waters of Babylon*, is about a sleazy East European brothel owner who gets mixed up in a plot to fiddle a municipal lottery; an Irish pimp and a West Indian tart discuss their recruiting drive on his behalf:

BATHSHEBA: Two today from Trinidad and there was one from Jamaica. I brought them along for to see Mr. Krank. Will he keep them, maybe? No, I don't know. Not what I'd call real proud-jetting young women, not what I'd call flying fish or torpedoes. No sir, just kind of sad and quiet gentle seaweed laid out

dark on a cold hard beach. You've been along to
meet a train too?

CASSIDY: The Irish Mail, no less. And there they stepped
down from it, six beautiful doxies, Seaweed? – No
sea-weed but all roaring gorse, wild whitethorn, a
chiming tempest of girls, turned that dirty Euston
into a true windswept altitude, a crystal mountain-
top for love. Or for Mr. Krank's finances, which is
more to the purpose.

In the original script this is set out like free verse, but the
rhythms are plain enough in any case. There is certainly no
need to set it alongside a piece of 'naturalistic' dialogue to
point the difference. If it has a linguistic ancestor, it is
Under Milk Wood; but Dylan Thomas only put such a
wealth of simile and metaphor and such a build-up of
rhythmic energy into the mouths of characters acting as
narrators (whether the two formal 'Voices' who take us
round the village or the ordinary villagers who pause and
describe for us what they are doing at that moment). This
exchange, by contrast, is a conversation, in which the
subject may be a familiar one to the characters engaged in
it – but they are just as verbally lively when cleaning
lavatories or making love or discussing the IRA. What is
special about this kind of dialogue is the faith that it
implies – a faith in words themselves. Arden is writing in
an era in which the limits of language, the impossibility of
true communication, are almost taken for granted. The
conviction reaches its theatrical apotheosis in the work of
Beckett, grounded in the assumption that man is driven by
words but always let down by them, that 'there is nothing
to express, nothing from which to express, no power to
express, no desire to express, together with the obligation
to express'.[7] The conviction is also present in Pinter's early

27

plays, or in later ones like *Landscape* and *Silence* in which characters speak to themselves rather than to each other, and in which even the author does not know everything about them. (Pinter has mentioned that he only learned the identity of the 'man on the beach' in *Landscape* at the rehearsal stage.)[8]

It is even more interesting to look at Arden's dialogue in relation to a writer who appears to have considerable linguistic energy, and yet still manifests a real lack of faith in language. Take this extract from Osborne's *Look Back in Anger*:

JIMMY: She'd drop your guts like hair clips and fluff all over the floor. You've got to be fundamentally insensitive to be as noisy and as clumsy as that. I had a flat underneath a couple of girls once. You heard every damned thing those bastards did, all day and night. The most simple, everyday actions were a sort of assault course on your sensibilities. I used to plead with them. I even got to screaming the most ingenious obscenities I could think of, up the stairs at them. But nothing, nothing would move them. With those two, even a simple visit to the lavatory sounded like a medieval siege. Oh, they beat me in the end – I had to go. I expect they're still at it. Or they're probably married by now, and driving some other poor devils out of their minds. Slamming their doors, stamping their high heels, banging their irons and saucepans – the eternal flaming racket of the female. Oh hell! Now the bloody bells have started! Wrap it up, will you? Stop ringing those bells! There's somebody going crazy in here! I don't want to hear them!

ALISON: Stop shouting! You'll have Miss Drury up here.

JIMMY: I don't give a damn about Miss Drury – that mild old gentlewoman doesn't fool me, even if she takes in you two. She's an old robber. She gets more than enough out of us for this place every week. Anyway, she's probably in church, swinging on those bloody bells!

CLIFF: Come on now, be a good boy. I'll take us all out and we'll have a drink.

JIMMY: They're not open yet. It's Sunday. Remember? Anyway, it's raining.[9]

Jimmy is articulate, but perilously so. It is not simply that the energy of his tirades is purely negative; it also has to feed off others and is incapable of giving. The other characters only exist as straight men – both Alison and Cliff are here to provide new subject matter as he begins to flag. Because his language is parasitic, there is no possibility of dialogue. If, as Osborne implies, we are all articulate at one another's expense, speech is inevitably one-sided, with the verbal honours going to the fittest. It is clear, from Jimmy's use of words like 'sensibilities' and the 'fundamentally' beloved of essay-writers, that he is educated and therefore stands a good chance of getting a word in edgeways; but his speeches also carry with them a sense of their own futility, betrayed in the frequent use of words like 'anyway', and in their dependence on fantasy. Jimmy cannot deal with the here and now; instead he launches into more fertile linguistic ground with a few 'probably's or 'I expect's to keep himself going. He is in a kind of prison of language, beating against the bars.

The same can be said of Joe Orton's characters, who speak a language fantastically ornate but consisting entirely of clichés; and this in turn circumscribes what they do. They can only cope with the trivial and the flashy, because they don't have the words with which to conceive of anything better.

In the Arden extract, however, the characters betray no sign of strain or powerful emotion to fuel their tongues; this is simply the way they talk. Arden is of course aware that people do not talk like this (any more than they talk like Jimmy Porter); articulacy is a gift which he gives them, regardless of class, education, intelligence or nationality. In doing so he knocks on the head the concept of decorum which began with the Elizabethans; they insisted that a character should speak a language appropriate to his or her station in life – poetry for the upper classes, prose for the lower.

Decorum was of course often ignored and also often used very creatively; but the bloodless remains of the idea continued to hang around the theatrical subconscious, and eventually gave rise to the dreadful stage workmen and servants who prefaced every remark with 'Beggin' yer pardon, mum', of which Kenneth Tynan still complained in the 1950s. Arden instead goes straight back to the tradition of the medieval miracle play. Here, not only the saints and apostles but the nameless peasants, the shepherds and midwives and incense-vendors were as articulate as God himself. The Yorkshire sheep-herders who worship at the manger do so in verse charged with homely and beautiful imagery; Cain's boy reproves his master for Abel's murder in a style that equals God's in liveliness, if not in majesty. One reason for this is made plain in the play of the Last Judgement: the plays envisage the possibility of personal change; it is up to you whether you accept or reject salvation, whether you lead the kind of life that will take you to heaven or hell. The social structure of the Middle Ages did not permit mobility, but

30

in the spiritual one there was a sort of equality; it is always clear in the plays that even if characters like Judas have to speak the lines set down for them, the point of the whole cycle is to spell out the possibility of choice.

Similarly Arden's language is public, social. His characters inhabit a social structure which can be changed. This is made explicit in later plays, such as *The Ballygombeen Bequest*:

> When you act in a play it is easy to say
> That we shall win and never be defeated
> When you go from here it is not so clear
> That power for the people is predestined –
> Giddy-i-aye but don't forget
> Giddy-i-aye but you must remember
> Giddy-i-aye tiddle-iddle-oo
> There are more of us than them . . .

Here the invitation is plain; it is made to us, as well as to characters onstage, and it is an invitation to take up a specifically Marxist position. Even in the earliest plays, which do not take sides so plainly, characters move freely in their language and their society; they may be trapped by problems like poverty and prejudice, but they are not crippled imaginatively. The richness of the language makes everything seem possible, although Arden never shirks showing the cost of change.

It is an extremely rich language; all Arden's characters have huge vocabularies, dialect words from Yorkshire or Ireland, from medieval Scots and from languages even older – the shepherds in *The Business of Good Government* count their sheep using a numerical system so old its origins are lost – sonorous Latinate abstract nouns; verse and prose; speech and song. They are never defeated

31

by words; they can always say what they feel and think – to each other, and also directly to us; for it seems a corollary of their formidable articulacy that they should share it with us as fully as possible. Take, for instance, another speech in *The Waters of Babylon* in which the corrupt councillor, Charlie Butterthwaite, tells his life story to Krank the brothel-owner:

As a young lad I began in Trades Union Offices.
Railways, smoke, black steel, canals, black stone.
That were my town, and where sets the power?
Mill owners: I saw that. Hundredweights of them.
Murky money. But not for me, not for our Charlie.
Conjure up the adverse power from out the
crowded smoke:
Union Headquarters. Only a young lad; I begin: I go on:
From Union on to Council, Councillor to Alderman,
Alderman to Mayor, unfolded power of scarlet
broadening back and belly: but that weren't the secret:
it's not gold chain nor scarlet carries right power.
Committees. Chairman of this one, secretary of that one,
Housing Development, Chamber of Trade,
Municipal Transport, Hospitals, Welfare Amenities.
Eat your Christmas dinners in the Lunatic Asylum,
Colliery Canteens, in the poor old Borough Orphanage,
Weekly photo in the paper in a paper hat and all
Cheery Charlie Butterthwaite; there was puddings to
them dinners.

Although Krank gives him a rather crude cue for the speech 'You fascinate me', it is clear that we will only be fascinated by the speech if it is plainly shared with us; Krank's reactions will not be of much interest – it seems inevitable that he's going to get involved with Charlie, speech or no speech. Charlie is telling *us* the story, giving us a taste of his quality and the world he moves in, inviting us to judge him and it. It will be a complex judgement, as like most of the main characters in Arden's early plays he is a mixture of good and bad, but he will not hinder the process by hiding from us and forcing us to search for subtextual clues.

Brecht once praised a production of Gorki's *Mother* because the lines 'were properly spoken . . . with the same sense of responsibility as a statement made for the record in a court of law'.[10] Charlie is not a socially responsible character – his career in local government has been adequately chequered before his dubious antics with the lottery – but the style of his speech has the quality Brecht admired; it sets him in a very clear social context, spelt out in solid terms – puddings and steel, flesh and smoke – and outlining a very definite power-structure. It indicates the attitudes of the men who manipulate the structure – Charlie chooses words like 'the adverse power' to show that, to the men inside it, it is as powerful as the crowns and dukedoms of Italy to a Jacobean tragic hero. This in turn implies other and better ways of using the structure for socially desirable ends – although Arden never loses sight of the paradox that men like Charlie really do accomplish a great deal through their dishonest wheeling and dealing – 'there was puddings to them dinners'. Arden's verse always keeps us aware of a whole society, which includes ourselves; and, however complex that verse, it often grounds itself in the most basic imagery of food and clothing to make its point.

Before moving from Arden's use of words it might be useful to look at an example of his use of ballad in a very pure form. It is somewhat crude compared to the delicacy he was later to achieve, but in its context it works

powerfully. In *The Waters of Babylon* Krank is asked by
Bathsheba to sing what he calls his Dolorous Song:

> As I went down by Belsen town
> I saw my mother there
> She said go by, go by, my son, go by
> But leave with me here
> Your lovely yellow hair.
>
> As I went down by Auschwitz town
> My brother looked out of the wall
> He said go by, go by, my brother, go by
> But leave with me here
> The lovely strong tooth from your skull.
>
> As I went down by Buchenwald town
> And there for my sweetheart I sought
> But she whispered go by, Oh my darling go by
> You leave with me here
> The lovely red blood of your heart.

The song has a complex effect. It uses the triadic structure
and imagery of folk song – the red blood, the yellow hair –
and it is sung to a folk tune: I heard it sung to the tune *The
Leaves of Life*, a song about the Redemption which
formed an ironic counterpoint to the words. The pain
which many folk songs take as their subject is generally
distanced, or at least contained by, the stylized imagery,
and at first sight the song might seem to be casting a kind
of romantic-historical glow over the concentration camps.
But the actual names of those camps in their un-
compromising reality force upon us also the remem-
brance that in them the hair and teeth and bones of
the song were treated as commodities, that they do not

refer to some generalized notion of a beautiful person with nice features but to a real human being who could be reduced by the Nazi war-machine to an inventory of potentially usable parts. So a tension is set up between the romantically stylized and the painfully specific, rendered all the more powerful in performance by the contrast between the lovely tune and the harsh East European accent of Krank.

The song is also sung in a context, and this makes its effect even more complicated. In the first place, it is sung by Krank, a man towards whom our feelings are made to fluctuate violently; he is a pimp and a cheat; then we are told that he was in Buchenwald; we grow to like him, just as he is liked by all the girls who work for him; then we find out that he was a guard in the camp; but at once he makes a speech which challenges our right to judge anyone in his situation. But Arden is not looking for sympathy for Krank; he wants us to look at a whole society. Krank, Bathsheba, Teresa, the West Indian councillor Joe Caligula, Cassidy and the Polish fanatic Paul are all strangers in a foreign land, the post-war London in which Harold Macmillan made his famous pronouncement 'You've never had it so good' and set off a scramble for the material goodies the war had made unobtainable for many years, while race riots and slum landlords darkened the face of the apparent optimism. The song shows one of the foundations of that society, the legacy of the war. For some, this is one of pure bitterness: Paul wants to blow up the visiting Russian delegation, Henry Ginger is infected with fascism. Some have forgotten it altogether. Bathsheba's comment on the song is 'Man, you must have travelled wide,' and this innocence makes her vulnerable; Joe sees her as a symbol of all the mistreated immigrants in London 'told go down, go down, here is enough warmth and light already, you are come among us uncalled-for, as smoke and shadows to drench out our fire in an alien ugliness'. For Krank, the war must be remembered even though his own part in it was discreditable. All these responses to a political fact are suddenly crystallized in one song.

Arden's use of space is also distinctive; he has used several different stage shapes and tried numerous spatial techniques of breaking down the barriers between actor and audience. In *Serjeant Musgrave's Dance*, for instance, the audience is treated like the crowd in the market-place and when the soldiers turn the Gatling gun upon the crowd it points directly in our faces; in the Royal Court this brought the gun very close indeed. *The Happy Haven* was designed for the small experimental theatre at Bristol University which had an open stage rather on Elizabethan lines; it blurred the distinction between actors and audience still further by following the colour scheme of the auditorium on the stage; there were local spatial jokes, too – the comic lecture in the play gained extra laughs because the building itself was used for lectures. And the uncluttered shape of the open stage made it easier for the actors to display the acrobatic energy and agility that counterpointed their roles as old people, so that we were forced to stand back and think about old age rather than about the characters. *Armstrong's Last Goodnight* also showed to best advantage on an Elizabethan type stage at the Chichester Festival Theatre where it received its first English performance. It made use of a medieval convention of 'mansions', that is, of three simultaneous settings, Castle, Palace and Wood. They vividly reflected three kinds of lifestyle and brought alive the dangers encountered on a journey among them.

The Business of Good Government made an even more

interesting use of space, using free movement between actors and audience in a way that involved them and yet provoked thought. It was played in a church. Some of the action resembled a religious service; at the beginning, for instance, the actors walked in procession up the nave singing a carol and, when not required in the action, they sat in the choir stalls. The Angel spoke from the pulpit the words that had been spoken there countless times: 'Behold, I bring you tidings of great joy which shall be to all people.' The birth of Jesus took place in the chancel, close to the altar. And, like the Christmas story itself, the play is starred with images of death and resurrection, of the cycle of nature, like the lullaby to the child Jesus:

> Go to sleep, little baby, and then you will see
> How strong grows the acorn on the branches of the tree.
>
> How tightly it lives in the green and the brown
> But the strong storms of autumn will soon shake it down.
>
> The deeper it falls then the stronger will it tower
> Bold roots and wide limbs and a true heart of power.
>
> Though the oak is the master of all the trees on the hill
> His heart will be mastered by the carpenters will.

These images, superimposed as they were in Margaretta D'Arcy's production upon the familiar cruciform shape of the church and surrounded by all the normal trappings of worship, become a kind of version of the Creed. Thus the audience have a sensation of being participants rather than observers; they join in a celebration and an act of worship. But the close, informal contact between actors and audience also makes it possible for them to be confronted by the action and made to question it. The hostess at the 'inn' tells us about the experience of living in an occupied country and the stress caused by the census, and we see her offer of the stable in a new light; it is an act of harried kindness rather than a callous rejection of Joseph and Mary. Herod speaks directly to us about his struggle to placate the powerful nations on his doorstep and the need for unquestioned authority – so the Massacre of the Innocents is seen as a political choice, not gratuitous sadism, and we have to judge it as such. Consequently we see the story of the Nativity not simply as well-loved ritual, but as the product of specific decisions by people in complex situations. We have to think, guided by the presence of the Angel in the pulpit, just as we have to think when listening to a sermon; we judge the participants in the story, but we do not do so lightly. At the end of the play, we celebrate; the miraculous aspects of the story are presented joyfully, and the whole cast join in the closing carol, regardless of the parts they have taken, so that even the playing of Herod has become an act of reasoned worship.

This distinctive use of both space and language demands in turn a particular acting style, and Arden and D'Arcy have offered numerous hints as to its nature, in articles and essays, in practice, and also, by implication, in the plays themselves. It is plain that a naturalistic approach will usually be disastrous; the Vicar of Brent Knoll was nearer the mark when he assured his parishioners that they would not have to *act*, but to speak their lines as if reading the lesson. Although this ignores the many technical skills needed by an actor who plays in a typical Arden/D'Arcy work – dancing, tumbling and conjuring tricks have all featured from time to time – this is a good analogy. To read a lesson well involves direct communication of a story to its listeners; it demands an inner conviction of the truth of that story, but not identification with its characters, a hard-edged clarity that is a long way from coldness.

Arden does not want to absorb his audience but to hold a dialogue with them. Sometimes, indeed, the actors must speak the lines in such a way as to invite judgment on their characters. This is striking in *Armstrong's Last Goodnight*. Gilnockie has been hanged in our sight, singing the ballad of his deeds that the play dramatizes. As the play ends the man responsible, Lindsay, and his lady, who has slept with Gilnockie, and Gilnockie's wife share an image which they recite to us:

LINDSAY: There was ane trustless tale grew out of this conclusion –

WIFE: That the tree on whilk he was hangit spread neither leaf nor blossom –

LADY: Nor bloom nor sap within its branches –

LINDSAY: Frae this time forth and for evermair. It did fail and it did wither upon the hill of Carlanrigg, as ane dry exemplar to the world. Here ye may read the varieties of dishonour, and determine in your mind how best ye can avoid whilk ane of them, and when . . .

They are neither in nor out of character. Lindsay has shown in the play that he considers himself justified in his betrayal; the women have been more intimately involved, less concerned with Gilnockie as political force. Here they in effect finish the ballad he sang at his death and failed to finish, the ballad which in its original version presents Gilnockie as most foully betrayed. Lindsay juxtaposes this view with his own, with words like 'trustless' and 'dry exemplar', but he is nonetheless participating in a ballad that takes a different view of his behaviour. We must judge for ourselves, and the Lindsay actor must be sure not to colour his speech with suggestions of either triumph or remorse.

Gareth Lloyd Evans once remarked perceptively that the lines of Shaw needed to be spoken with candour, that the actors should look squarely at one another with their eyes in contact. There is a similar quality in Arden; both word and act require a kind of honesty in their delivery, even those uttered by characters like Butterthwaite and Krank. Arden's dislike of the kind of verse used in plays like *The Cocktail Party*, which slithers coyly out of prose and back again, is significant; his verse is unashamed. This honesty extends to physical acts as well. The word 'upright' occurs many times to describe the stance of characters. Pearl, for instance, sees herself in the mirror 'bolt-upright' and she later says that this is how she will play the brave Queen Esther, standing fearlessly before the king to save her people. 'Straight' is a word constantly on the lips of Serjeant Musgrave, and his stance bears it out. Lindsay's lady provides us with a gently mocking description of Gilnockie: 'You are ane lovely lion to roar and leap, and sure wad rarely gratify all submissive ladies beneath the rampancy of your posture. Ye are indeed heraldic, sir.' Characters stand and move, but rarely sit. Typically, they enter as if shot from a gun, losing no time in establishing themselves and their function in the action. In *The Ballygombeen Bequest*, for instance, we are possessed of many salient facts in a few seconds:

HOLLIDEY-CHEYPE: Good evening, Hollidey-Cheype, at your service. Percival Hollidey-Cheype, Lieutenant Colonel, retired. Very recently retired.
Five minutes ago, in fact.

> Observe the nap upon my bowler hat.
> The war is over. That is that.

The music-hall vitality of this opening gets the play off to a fine start and launches the actor into a dialectical relationship with his audience. It also indicates the period, his social class and the attitude of that class to the war – it has ceased to matter because there is money to be made.

The 'bowler hat' with its new nap is a typical detail; throughout the plays costume is used with great care, an extension of the language. A speech by Lindsay expresses some of the force that garments carry in any Arden play:

> The rags and robes that we do wear
> Express the function of our life
> But the bawdy body that we bear
> Beneath them carries nocht
> But shame and grief and strife.

The frequent use of historical settings means that costumes will often be decorative and exotic. It is important, however, that these are not seen as a mere marzipan coating on the text; the preface to *The Island of the Mighty* says, 'The essential precept to bear in mind in dressing these plays is Lenin's famous question: "Who? Whom?" Who, for example, derives his income at the expense of whom, and how is this demonstrated in their personal appearance?' While this play is concerned with a period in which these distinctions could be clearly delineated, most of the plays demand clothes that express the social function of the characters. King John in *Left Handed Liberty* has a great deal to say about his crown and about the significance of a present from the Pope which proves to be silver-gilt and not gold. *Serjeant Musgrave's Dance* floods the stage with red coats to symbolize the final failure of the protest against war.

Armstrong's Last Goodnight uses costume to dramatize several kinds of conflict. First, there is that between two styles of life. Lindsay's own choice is a simple black suit, neat and smooth. Gilnockie's clothes and those of his men express their need to fight both men and weather; they wear skins and furs and leathers, linking them with the animals and reflecting their concern for their territory in the browns and greys that match the earth and forest. Secondly, there is the conflict between different roles adopted within these ways of life and the attitude of Gilnockie and Lindsay towards them. Gilnockie sees the trappings as expressing something about *himself.* He takes pride in the gilt collar that symbolizes his new role as King's Lieutenant. He dresses up to meet the king in a selection of gaudy clothes and glittering badges which suggest his jackdaw attitude to property and his lack of understanding of the court; they are an expression of his roaring ego, not his function. Lindsay, more sophisticated, understands that dress is essentially symbolic; his herald's tabard shows that he has a mission for the king. Its colour and stylized pattern show the more ordered society from which he springs. But it also implies a degree of dehumanization. The richness makes the fabric stiff. At Chichester, Lindsay looked like a Court card; the shortness of the tabard was the only indication of vulnerability, the legs remaining in their original black and looking slender and weak by contrast with the bulky upper part.

Armstrong's Last Goodnight also exploits the removal of clothing as an illustration of the conflict. Both Lindsay and Gilnockie reach states of symbolic nakedness, but here the roles are reversed. Lindsay does not understand its implications. He doffs his tabard at the start of the play in order to deal with Gilnockie 'as ane man against ane man' but he fails, and dons it again for the last betrayal as if trying to use his role as an excuse. He can never be 'ane man', whatever he is wearing, because he sees it as a role like any other. But Gilnockie's stripping dramatizes his strength as well as his simplicity:

> Here is ane brand. Aff.
> (*He drops belt and sword on the stage.*)
> Here's a gilt collar and ane title. Aff.
> (*He throws his collar down.*)
> Here is ane buft jacket of defence. Aff.
> (*He strips off his buff coat.*)
> Here is my gully. Out.
> (*He pulls his knife out of the top of his trunk-hose and drops it.*)
> I'm in my sark and my breeks wi' nae soldiers, nae horses. As there were no soldiers wi' David Lindsay, when he stood before my yett. Am accoutrit convenient for ane passage of love. Or for execution. Or what else?

In his courageous and genuine vulnerability he assumes that everyone makes the same gesture for the same reasons. He is capable of criminal deceit – the play opens with a treacherous murder at his behest – but he also equates nakedness and truth. Diplomatic nakedness is beyond his understanding and beneath his contempt.

Arden frequently uses the symbol of nakedness. In *Pearl* we have two kinds of nudity, that of Pearl looking at herself in the glass and understanding a truth about herself, her desire for the theatre, and that of Pearl stripped by her enemies to blind the audience to the truth of her play and bring it into lascivious discredit. The same symbol is used differently in *The Workhouse Donkey*, in which the costumes of the strippers are sleazy and stupid, trivializing sex with bells and balloons, and yet simultaneously suggest the possibility of genuine eroticism. Arden was foiled in this aim at Chichester, as the sensibilities of the Lord Chamberlain forced the actresses to wear rather substantial costumes which made the idea of a police raid on the strip club somewhat bewildering.

Arden's concern for the visual aspects of the theatre is also seen in his frequent use of masks. He first tried them in *The Happy Haven*, the first play co-written with Margaretta D'Arcy. They were part of the comic mode of the play that called for wild energy from the young actors playing old people, the chases and conjuring tricks that allowed laughter at the ludicrous plot while balancing it with very clear and simple questions about the real fate of old people forced into homes which treat them as fools or scientific guinea-pigs. Albert Hunt worked on the play some years after its original production, and the masks he produced with the help of Arden and D'Arcy were far more exaggerated than those used in 1960. The most powerful and surrealistic masks Arden and D'Arcy have used so far, however, were made for *The Non-Stop Connolly Show*. It employed a basic pattern mask adapted in various ways. Some were given extra features to resemble specific political figures; all the capitalists had bilious greeny-yellow creations which made clear the links between them. The 'villain of the piece' was a figure with the composite name Grabitall, who sometimes acted as a general Demon King of the Right and sometimes represented real people. In the last part of the play he was William Martin Murphy. By this time, however, the mask had gathered all kinds of sinister connotations from previous plays in the cycle and so provided a focus for the final struggle, a symbol of oppression for us and the tiring Connolly. The most memorable masks of all, though, were those of the War Demons. They were sufficiently like the others to demonstrate the inevitable links between war and the capitalist system, but surrounded by flame-like projections that suggested those used in a war dance. They underlined the idea of war as a dreadful *force* which could be controlled by men for their own ends, rather than as a simple clash of armies.

As Arden pointed out in a subsequent lecture on masks, the mask enforces a particular style on actors. They must deliver their lines to the audience rather than to one another – a mask has to be seen from the front, not the side – and this can give rise to a clear, direct and powerful delivery, which can serve political drama well. He cited an instance when members of the Galway Theatre Workshop staged a musical protest wearing faceless white hoods, which caused unprecedented alarm on the part of local councillors and police. It is a theatrical device to which he may well turn increasingly in political plays, and one whose unique excitement he handles skilfully.

Masks almost inevitably involve the use of songs and dance. Arden's songs are not there solely because they contribute to the analysis of the situation, but also for their own sake. He employs all the resources of the actor: *The Workhouse Donkey* has a striptease, *Serjeant Musgrave's Dance* a clog dance by the colliers, *Armstrong's Last Goodnight* a lively country dance to the bagpipes. These should all be exercises of real skills which the audience can enjoy: Shakespeare's audience would see a dance within the play in this way and it undermines the plays if the dances are seen as a slightly embarrassing moment to be got over quickly. Arden uses, too, the physical vocabulary of the clown. There is a Fred Karno sequence in *Serjeant*

Musgrave's Dance in which the colliers solemnly but drunkenly practise drill, a routine with an imaginary dog in *The Happy Haven* and a custard pie fight in *The Ballygombeen Bequest*. Arden's determination to use every theatrical possibility available is really one aspect of his extraordinary energy.

To honesty, clarity and skill it is necessary for the Arden actor to add another attribute, something that might be called generosity. At the Edinburgh Drama Conference in 1963 Arden stated that 'The god of the theatre is and always has been Dionysus.'[11] In his preface to *The Workhouse Donkey* he outlined the prime qualities of the Dionysiac theatre:

> noise
> disorder
> drunkenness
> lasciviousness
> nudity
> generosity
> corruption
> fertility
>   and
> ease.

Many of his plays end with a song or celebration, and Albert Hunt has written about the most successful performance he ever staged of *Ars Longa Vita Brevis* which turned into a party.[12] It is interesting to note that this celebration is often in defiance of logic; the carol at the end of *The Business of Good Government* is a deliberate assertion of the miraculous in the face of a world that can order the Massacre of the Innocents; the rich property developers have won at the end of *The Ballygombeen*

Bequest, but the ghost of Padraic gaily sets up the custard pies and reminds us that the fight can still go on. The vitality is anarchic in spirit; it does not arise out of events, but is generated by the richness of the style and the communication achieved with the audience, by the frank theatricality – and by the characters.

Although they are conceived in terms of their public roles and functions rather than in psychological detail, this does not mean that Arden's characters are devoid of individuality; most of their individuality in fact arises from the quality of their energy. Musgrave, for instance, can set the stage alight with the wildness of his dance, a wildness that comes from the sudden liberation of the energy he has hitherto expended in mental and physical rigidity. Gilnockie is charged with the energy of egotism. A task Arden set himself while at Bristol, the translation of Goethe's first play *Goetz Von Berlichingen*, suggests that he has been at pains to explore the whole idea of a 'hero' and the energies implied by the word. The play, written when Goethe was only twenty-four, has all the vitality associated with the early Romantic movement – but also a certain naive acceptance of the central figure at his own valuation. In his own version, *Ironhand*, Arden set about strengthening the role of Goetz's opponent Weislingen. His comment on this is interesting:

> To a poet bored to death with the polite decorum of pre-revolutionary European society, the life led by such men as Goetz, with their Gothic castles, their armour, their bands of hard-riding, hard-drinking horse-troopers etcetera, must have seemed one of unalloyed excitement. But the very intelligence and imagination with which Goethe captures the personalities and events of his story make us refuse to accept his romantic view

of them. Goetz in particular lives so strongly as a man that in justice to him and his creator some sort of judgement must be made upon his actions.

This comment reflects the advice of Marx to Lasalle, who was trying to write a play on the same subject, but with a different hero. The figure of Goetz is an anachronism; he doesn't fit into the social order of his time, but neither does he fit into a state ruled by and for the people; and yet his energy and vitality make him the only possible hero.[13] It is a useful *caveat* for anyone watching an Arden play; it is sometimes, though not always, necessary to dissociate the attractiveness of the life force from the characters who possess it or the ends to which they use it. Not to do so is to treat them as 'tragic heroes' in the Aristotelian mould, figures destroyed by a fatal flaw for whom we should feel pity. This view was put forward in a programme note to the National Theatre's production of *Armstrong's Last Goodnight*, describing the Arden hero as:

> not the rebel who withdraws to the other side to oppose, but instead remains involved in, and corrupted by, a society which he has come to loathe; a person who, in the end, has become the epitome of the corrosive society which has made him, until, finally aware of the nature of that society through himself, he tries to destroy both it and himself. It is a figure that is essentially of the twentieth century, the figure of Everyman equipped with huge energy, but refusing, in the last lurch of self-loathing and wilfulness, to control it.[14]

In fact few of Arden's heroes loathe themselves. Goetz's last word is 'freedom'; Gilnockie dies singing; Nelson, in

The Hero Rises Up, has qualms about the way he is posthumously idolized, but smothers them in the general rejoicing. Charlie Butterthwaite ends *The Workhouse Donkey* with a triumphant recital of his achievements: 'Oh, oh, oh, I have lived, I have controlled, I have redistributed. The Commonwealth has gained. The tables have been spread. Not with bread and marge, you know, like they used to in the workhouse, but with a summation of largesse demanding for its attendance soup-spoons in their rank, fish-knives and forks, flesh-knives and forks, spoons for the pudding . . .' The recital eventually rises to an assertion of loony divinity:

> . . . In my rejection I have spoken to this people. I will rejoice despite them. I will divide Dewsbury and mete out the valley of Bradford; Pudsey is mine, Huddersfield is mine, Rotherham also is the strength of my head, Ossett is my lawgiver, Black Barnsley is my washpot, over Wakefield will I cast out my shoe, over Halifax will I triumph. Who will bring me into the strong city, who will lead me into the boundaries of Leeds? Wilt thou not, oh my deceitful people, who hast cast me off? And wilt not thou go forth with Charlie?

He decks himself with flowers and a tablecloth like a Lord of Misrule or a comic King Lear, singing a song whose content may be a lament for the 'poor old donkey' but which has a jaunty tune of which Arden demands a fortissimo reprise after he has been finally ejected from the theatre. We are asked not to mourn his downfall but to celebrate the energy that led up to it, an energy which sparkles through the play like an almost tangible force. Sometimes, indeed, it is there *between* characters rather than as part of them.

Arden continually celebrates sexual energy as a force which has in itself enough power to threaten the social order. His love scenes often bear a distinct resemblance to spells. Bathsheba and Joe Caligula make love in rhymed couplets which evolve into full-blown ritual:

CALIGULA: No.

BATHSHEBA: No? Draw a circle, walk it round.

CALIGULA (*beginning to be caught*) Draw a circle on the ground. Say I was the lantern and you was the dark.

BATHSHEBA: You could thrust at me though, wherever I'd lurk.

The Lady in *Armstrong's Last Goodnight* causes Gilnockie to lose the impediment in his speech as she seduces him. When she articulates her own power it is in hypnotic verse whose imagery recalls the magic cauldrons of Celtic myth which never stopped their flow of food:

There is in me ane knowledge, potent, secret
That I can set to rin ane sure concourse
Of bodily and ghaistly strength betwixt the blood
Of me and of the starkest man alive. My speed
Hangs twin with yours: and starts ane double flood.
Will you with me initiate the deed
And saturatit consequence thereof – ?
Crack off with your great club
The barrel-hoops of love
And let it pour
Like the enchantit quern that pours red-herring broo
Until it gars upswim the goodman's table and his door
While all his house and yard and street
Swill reeken, greasy, het, oer-drownit sax-foot fou –

The speech is like a microcosm of an entire Arden play. It is lyrical and yet grounded in the most basic and homely things, the basics of survival. It is opulent and generous. It challenges the present order of things. In this case, it brings about a beneficent change. In his preface to *Plays One*, which include *Armstrong's Last Goodnight*, Arden wondered whether he would ever again write stage-plays of quite this kind.[15] He has certainly worked in very different kinds of theatre since, and has continued to question all our preconceptions about what theatre is, and whom it is for. The determination to stretch actor and audience to the limit of their resources, both physical and intellectual, and the energy which informs his work, however, remain.

3
Manner

I will make my love this image to love
And upon its hard brow I will write:
'This dream is my love yet you are my love
And who can tell which in the night?'
(John Arden, *I'll make my love a Breast of Glass*)

In Ben Jonson's play *Bartholomew Fair* the self-righteous
Puritan Zeal-of-the-Land-Busy attacks the little puppet
show on the grounds that the theatre is licentious and
corrupt; he is refuted triumphantly by one of the puppets
pulling up his costume to reveal that they are quite sexless
and therefore quite innocent. The scene typifies Jonson's
use of self-conscious theatricality. Most of us experience
the idea of the play-within-the-play through Shakespeare,
in *Hamlet* or *A Midsummer Night's Dream*. Here it is a
way of investigating the role of the imagination; actors and
audience alike turn from the play to the consciousness that
life itself is a play or dream, and the theatre is its mirror.

Jonson, however, uses the same device as a means of analysis; the theatre is a tool or a microscope. At the beginning of *Bartholomew Fair* a contract is drawn up: the author promises to entertain the audience, and they promise to think for themselves. This is very much like the unspoken contract between Arden and his audience; it is not surprising to find that Jonson has been a major influence on his work.

Arden first encountered Jonson's work at George Devine's Edinburgh production in 1950; he describes himself as consciously looking at the time for a 'pattern-book', a set of clear instructions by a master craftsman about the construction of plays, as he was all too aware that the kind of plays he wanted to write were very different from those of the British theatre of 1950. What attracted him was the enormous zest with which Jonson controlled his huge cast, the very precise ear for everyday speech combined with the wild inventiveness that gave birth to a whole gallery of eccentrics, 'each of them, one way or another, as cracked as an old carrot'.[1] Jonson made nonsense of the distinction, which, as Arden observes, critics still insist on drawing, between popular theatre and a theatre of ideas. He used slapstick and dirty jokes in plays whose moral seriousness was clear and strong. He also possessed a wealth of learning with which to back up the arguments he put forward about both the manner and the matter of his theatre. And, like Arden, he often found himself called upon to justify his craft in print.

The adjective 'Jonsonian' frequently appears in Arden criticism. Tynan prophesied a 'full-scale Jonsonian satire'[2] on the strength of *The Waters of Babylon* with its combination of social comment and wild fantasy. Lindsay Anderson recalls that he described *The Workhouse Donkey* as 'like one of those awful subplots in Jacobean plays that never get anywhere', only to find that Arden was absolutely delighted. Arden is concerned to ground his work in the bedrock of British theatrical tradition. Jonson represents a high peak of that tradition, in that he wrote for an audience which embraced all classes of society and which accepted with equal pleasure the slapstick and the debate, the moral earnestness and the poetry. Arden has shown the breakdown of that classless audience in *Pearl*; in some of his experiments in community theatre he has made some attempt to restore it.

The other English-speaking playwright of whom Arden speaks with much warmth is Sean O'Casey; he has written several essays on O'Casey's work and, in collaboration with Margaretta D'Arcy, presented a television script, *Portrait of a Rebel*, in 1973. Some of the attraction he feels towards O'Casey can be found in the most popular plays: *Juno and the Paycock*, *Shadow of a Gunman* and *The Plough and the Stars* have the same vernacular vitality Arden admired in Jonson. They also use the techniques of knockabout farce to express sober truths about the society they portray; as Samuel Beckett once perceptively remarked, the knockabout begins with the furniture but it is also at work in the spiritual and social planes.[3] The later plays, some of the most underestimated in English language drama, have also influenced Arden profoundly. In an essay written in 1975 he expounded their special qualities and the importance he attaches to them.

Arden saw O'Casey as working within the tradition whose theatrical disintegration he describes in *Pearl*, but which was taken up by Bunyan in *Pilgrim's Progress*: that is the morality play tradition in which actors simultaneously represented spiritual states and political realities. Thus in Lindsay's *Three Estates* the protagonist is Humanity, over whom Chastity and Sensuality fight – but he is also a King, aided in his eventual victory over the Vices by a character called John the Commonweal. In the Elizabethan history cycles, the Virtues and Vices become further humanized, into Henry VI or Joan la Pucelle. After Cromwell the tradition moved into print, but the principle was the same. 'Vanity Fair, for instance, is of course a stage of sin wherein we are all liable to fall: but it is also London, with its theatres and brothels and taverns: and it is clearly presided over by a roaring Tory junta with Judge Jeffries on the bench.'[4]

This structure, Arden believes, was O'Casey's basic pattern-book for his political and social plays, and led him away from naturalism and into an essentially emblematic style, one which may be conceived in simple primary colours but which works very precisely indeed. O'Casey draws upon the Bible and upon Irish myth to give himself a complex iconography with which to work. His visual effects are calculated with great care, although they are not hard to achieve in the theatre. Arden cites the detailed instructions about colour he gives in the fourth act of *Red Roses for Me*, which demand a sharp juxtaposition of hues that must be given their full value at the expense of a naturalistic treatment of light and shade, and describes a production which ignored them and blunted its own political impact as a result. 'It looked non-committal: and in the end it was non-committal. Maybe if it hadn't been someone would have blown up the Lyric.'[5] Arden's own search for a clear emblematic style has been apparent since the precise visual conception in *Serjeant Musgrave's Dance*; his later decision to present a clear political position in his work will, perhaps, bring him still closer to the later O'Casey. Certainly there are echoes of *Cock-a-Doodle-Dandy* in the stylized bird mime in *The Non-Stop Connolly Show*, although the cheery sexuality of the

55

O'Casey play is closer in spirit to *The Workhouse Donkey* than to the dark parable of King Conaire; and the mixture of farce and ferocity in *The Ballygombeen Bequest*, with its scathing presentation of English exploitation of Irish land, may owe something to *Purple Dust*.

Arden is sadly aware that the techniques O'Casey spent a lifetime developing were never fully understood or realized in the theatre; he fitted neither into the orthodoxies of Marxist social-realism nor into the commercial theatre. One hopes that Arden does not foresee a similar fate for himself. It is, however, pleasant to record that the writer who has so profoundly influenced and entertained him stated that 'Serjeant Musgrave's Dance is far and away the finest play of the present day'.[6]

Jonson, O'Casey and most of the authors Arden has admired and learned from – Dickens, Lorca, Synge, Malory and his own contemporary Henry Livings among them – have all worked within the emblematic tradition. It was a tradition which, Arden felt, would keep the theatre alive. One of the more depressing aspects of the 1950s was the closure of numerous local repertory theatres; most of the blame was laid at the door of television, which was now within the reach of an increasing number of families. The most popular television plays were those which dealt with everyday life in a very naturalistic (although extremely bowdlerized) manner. Arden felt that the theatre was in danger of trying to beat television on its own ground, that many playwrights such as Wesker were trying to draw audiences back by using the same technique to present issues which were more challenging and important. In an article in *New Theatre Magazine* he dealt with the possible consequences of this strategy – that television will show up stage naturalism for the artificial creation it is and finish the theatre altogether. He argued that the theatre should, instead, concentrate on what it can do best and create an 'artificial' and unashamedly emblematic reality. 'People must', he argued, 'want to come to the theatre *because* of the artificiality, not in spite of it.'[7]

Later that same year, 1960, Arden wrote a short essay in *Encore* which has deservedly been reprinted many times and is perhaps the closest he ever came to a manifesto about his choice of language and style. *Telling a True Tale*, despite its brevity, repays a good deal of attention. Running like a ground bass through the essay is a sense of our very rich linguistic past. Arden does not mention the name of F. R. Leavis, but it seems very unlikely that he never heard him speak at Cambridge; even if he did not, it would be almost impossible to write an essay of this kind without some reference to one of Leavis's main beliefs – in a rich and largely rural culture in England's past, where speech was not only an art but one practised by the majority of the populace, so that Shakespeare and Bunyan were natural and organic products of their community – and a corresponding conviction that increasing industrialization has eroded this culture to a virtually irreparable degree.

Arden's position is more optimistic; while he feels that there is some truth in 'the modern idea of a sludgy uninterested nation, married to its telly and its fish and chips'[8], he also feels that this can be changed and that playwrights are in a position to do this. Their task, as he sees it, is to present the world as it is to their audience; his own method of presentation is essentially poetic: 'What I am deeply concerned with is the problem of translating the concrete life of today into terms of poetry that shall at the one time both illustrate that life and set it within the historical and legendary tradition of our culture.'[9] This desire takes Arden quite naturally back to what he sees as the 'bedrock' of English poetic tradition, that of the ballad. The ballads are the oral culture of the people: the matter they deal with is the most basic of all; they are about survival, about birth and death and resurrection; they are often grotesque, often violent, and, as Arden points out, extraordinarily anarchic. He is anxious to rescue the word 'tradition' from the popular connotations it had acquired in the 50s. To most people it carried overtones of the Royal Family and the last night of the Proms and everything the New Wave playwrights felt was wrong with Britain – John Osborne published his famous 'Damn you, England' letter in *Tribune*[10] almost simultaneously with *Telling a True Tale*. The real strength of the ballads, as Arden sees them, is that they combine an intensely felt life with a structure which can support any weight of meaning; we are, in fact, back to the idea of the craftsman's pattern-book.

The implications of this return to bedrock for the theatre are profound. Arden sees the logical structure for a poetic theatre as grounded in the Brechtian ideal: a hard, clear, honest style, in which verse is verse and prose is prose, in which the acting is naked and direct and uncluttered. An analogy Arden suggests is that of the oral bardic tradition:

The ancient Irish heroic legends were told at dinner as prose tales, of invariable content but, in the manner of their telling, improvised to suit the particular occasion or the poet's mood. When, however, he arrived at one of the emotional climaxes of the story such as the lament of Deirdre for the Sons of Usna or the sleep-song of Grainne over Diarmaid, then he would sing a poem which he had by heart and which was always the same. So in a play, the dialogue can be naturalistic and 'plotty' as long as the basic poetic issue has not been crystallised. But when this point is reached, then the language becomes formal (if you like, in verse or sung), the visual pattern coalesces into a vital image that is one of the nerve-centres of the play.[11]

This concept of poetic theatre is very different from that of, say, T. S. Eliot or Christopher Fry; they were, more or less, committed to the theatre of the magic box, imposing the idea of verse upon a pre-existing structure. Arden is looking for a radical transformation of the theatre and the most commonly accepted acting style. He is also proclaiming his faith in the theatre as a force for social change. Although his work at this stage was not overtly *political* in content, it raised a number of *social* issues; and Arden was in no doubt about the way in which the theatre should deal with social criticism. A documentary approach, he felt, had little ultimate effect; it moved people at the time and was then forgotten. On the other hand, the traditional poetic structures gave it a shape that would bestow force and dignity. A writer should never be afraid of being hackneyed in his choice of one of these themes, because their strength will allow of an infinite variety of treatment: 'There is scarcely any limit to the amount of meaning and relevance a writer can insert into them.'[12]

Telling a True Tale is to Arden's work what the *Preface to Lyrical Ballads* was to that of the early Wordsworth. There is the same belief in the strength of the 'bedrock' of the ballad tradition and the same determination to use that tradition to make the audience see life in a new way. There is also the same implied link between the attempt to change the accepted face of poetry and drama and the attempt to change society as a whole. Arden also assumes – mindful, perhaps, of the original reception of *Lyrical Ballads* – that he will be widely misunderstood by audiences with a firm idea of what theatre ought to be. It is interesting, then, that he should have chosen to discuss the idea of theatricality in a play for children, *The Royal Pardon*, written with Margaretta D'Arcy for the Beaford festival. It grew out of bedtime stories which they told to their own children, and its success at Beaford suggests that an audience free from preconceptions has very little trouble with the ideas adumbrated in *Telling a True Tale*. The play certainly makes no attempt to write down to its audience; in their preface, Arden and D'Arcy point out that children have no real objection to being occasionally puzzled by events in a play, just as they are sometimes puzzled by events in real life; and the analysis of the nature of theatre which they present is both subtle and challenging.

The central figure of *The Royal Pardon* is, like many Arden heroes, a soldier, Luke. He has deserted in Flanders and is arrested by the Constable; he escapes and joins a band of strolling players, also venomously pursued by the Constable as rogues and vagabonds; but the scenery Luke builds for the players is so good that they receive a royal pardon and a chance to represent England at the wedding of the English prince to the French princess. They all go off to France, the Constable in hot pursuit. Here the jealous French actors give the English company a poisoned tea; Luke and the utility girl, Esmeralda, who are so lowly that they aren't given any, are the only members of the company well enough to act; they stage an impromptu show in which the Constable gets hopelessly mixed up with the action and is finally turned to stone by Esmeralda wearing a gorgon-mask. The company wins the prize and the prince offers them a large government subsidy; the leading actors accept happily, but Luke and Esmeralda have other plans:

We two will attempt together a far more dangerous thing.
We will travel, hand in hand,
Across water and dry land –
We will entertain the people.

Arden and D'Arcy have in recent years done just that,
turning their backs on the subsidized theatres and opting
for a different kind of drama. This is not important in
itself – life does very frequently imitate art, after all – but
it does serve to underline the seriousness of the play's
concern with theatre values.

The play opens with a little song:

> Sun and moon and stars and rainbow
> Drum and trumpet, tambourine,
> A greedy king or a haughty beggar
> A virgin slut or a painted queen –
> Put your boots on, mask your faces
> Heave your cloaks and swing your swords,
> Laugh and weep and stamp with anger,
> Kick your jigs and strut the boards,
> All is painted, all is cardboard
> Set it up and fly away
> The truest word is the greatest falsehood,
> Yet all is true and all in play –
> Sun and moon and stars and rainbow
> Drum and trumpet, tambourine.

The song reflects the essential paradox of the theatre – that
truth can only be told through artificiality, and that a
healthy imagination accepts and enjoys the fact. The
Beaford production reflected this; actors and audience
were jammed together in close proximity and there was no
attempt to create an 'illusion'; the actors wore jeans and

61

plimsolls clearly visible beneath their costumes. Music was very important; in the rehearsal period a kind of musical counterpoint to the action was evolved by Boris and Russell Haworth, but there was no attempt to disguise the presence of the musicians; in fact, they became a visually exciting feature of the production, sitting inside a kind of polygonal cage of dowelling festooned with instruments of all kinds – drums, bells, cymbals, banjo, guitar, whistles and homemade items such as pottery cups tuned to different notes. The whole effect was cheap, intimate and cheerful.

The relationship between the real and the artificial is explored on many levels, but in a playful style. For instance, the Constable manages to convince himself through several ludicrous misunderstandings that the French princess is Luke in disguise and that the Prince is one of the players; he knocks the crown from the Prince's head saying triumphantly, 'Cardboard. You can't fool me. I know a theatrical property when I see one'. But as the crown lands on the floor it makes a loud clang.

The point is, of course, that the crown really is made of cardboard, very evidently so; and the clang is produced by a musician striking a cymbal in full view of the audience. Our enjoyment depends upon a simultaneous awareness and acceptance of theatricality. Similarly, the Constable responds to the trouser-splitting routine of the Clown with a shocked 'Children might have been present' – thus sharing an in-joke with what is, perhaps, the majority of the audience.

This juggling with different levels of reality is great fun; but the way in which people respond to theatre becomes, in the play, a kind of moral touchstone. There are many different attitudes displayed and they all betray a great deal about the characters who strike them. The theatrical style of the Crokes and the French company, for instance, is stuffy and overblown. Marcus Antonius Croke, the head tragedian and Luke's boss, struts and booms and rolls his eyes, assuring everyone that this is in the best classical tradition. At the same time he is tiresomely literal-minded; when, in rehearsal, he has to pluck a rose from a trellis and hand it to Guinevere, he refuses to go on unless both the trellis and the rose are instantly supplied. Theatre, for him, is not about imagination, but prestige. He is too snobbish to allow Luke to eat with the company, and only too delighted to accept the patronage of the King even though it is all too apparent that the King knows nothing at all about plays and only admires the Croke company because their scenery stays up in a high wind.

The two kings represent another way of looking at theatre. They are empty and trivial; the English King makes no bones of the fact that the only plays he really likes are those with jokes and women to look at. They cannot distinguish reality from illusion; when one of the English actors, under the influence of the poison, groans 'I feel a strange disturbance in my bowels', the French King complains about his language and assumes that his illness is part of the play. They are incapable of getting serious enjoyment from theatre, because in real life they are not interested in play but in deceit; both the prince and princess are warned by their fathers not to fall in love, because the marriage is only designed to patch up a quick peace while both sides prepare for war.

The most dangerous attitude of all, however, is that of the Constable; he hates the theatre and the players – 'no sense of morality or public decency whatever' – and so never really grasps the difference between the real and the unreal. Typically, he wants to arrest Luke for his *attempted* murder which he regards as far more serious than real murder. This narrow-mindedness makes him vulnerable. First he becomes part of the spectacle as he blunders onto the stage, and his pursuit of Luke makes the princess marvel at the energy and virility of English acting; then Luke manages to hypnotize him, significantly enough with a verse about the nature of illusion:

> Cardboard and paper and patches and glue
> Pleated and crumpled and folded in two
> With a pair of white fingers and a little bit of skill
> We make a whole world for the children to kill . . . .

He is turned to stone not by a real Gorgon but by Esmeralda in a very unconvincing mask which she has put on simply to hide the fact that she looks rather ill after her small share of the poisoned tea. It is rough, but undoubtedly poetic, justice.

The characters in *The Royal Pardon* who get most enjoyment from theatre are those who are most truthful in their own lives; the prince and princess take a zestful pleasure in Luke and Esmeralda's hasty improvisation; in their dealings with each other they have a direct sensual honesty that gives us a moment of theatrical excitement after all the courtly formality:

> PRINCE: . . . I must not fall in love. Neither must you.
> Nevertheless one flesh must be made out of our two
> (By the blessing of the Church): and by the blessing of good luck
> Yours and no-one else's is the fruit that I must pluck.
> Therefore, as I cram its fragrant pulp between my teeth
> Let me not pause for a moment's heedful breath –
> Let me tell myself rather 'Between this instant and my death

There can be no pleasure equal to what I now feel.
Let me not scatter peel nor pip nor core
Upon the ground to remind me that I could have
eaten yet more.

Luke himself has an even better instinctive understanding of theatre; although Arden and D'Arcy sometimes laugh at Luke – as when he selfrighteously claims that he didn't laugh at the Clown who has been entertaining the audience – he has clear and sound ideas about what he wants from a play. He criticizes the Crokes' play of St George and gives us his version of the story, in which the hero kills the dragon and then turns upon the King for sacrificing his own daughter without a fight. He wants a theatre which will faithfully reflect his own hard experience of life; when he has a chance to recite before the English King he takes the opportunity to tell the truth about the wars:

Starving though we were and tired and ill
We never did forget our soldier's skill:
We kept our boots clean and our bayonets bright,
We waved our banners and we marched upright,
We dared the French to meet us and to fight.
And when we met we fought till none could stand.
Our bodies now lie in a foreign land,
Defeated, they have said; but we know better:
We obeyed our general's orders to the letter.
If blame there is to be – indeed we did not win –
Blame not your loyal soldiers, gracious King,
But blame those ministers who, sitting warm at home
Sent us across the sea, unfed, unclothed, alone,
To do our duty the best way that we could.
We did it, sir, by pouring out our blood.
There is no more to say.

This, too, is an exciting moment in the play. Arden and D'Arcy seem to imply, especially through Luke, that real theatre is pretence which allows the truth to break in; Luke's descriptions of the hell of war and the almost violent lovemaking of the prince and princess are so powerfully real that one would half expect them to shatter the fabric of make-believe; instead, of course, they strengthen it. The moments of risk are necessary to test the fabric, and if the theatre does not take the risk of letting in the truth, it is not worth having. *The Royal Pardon* is a triumphant assertion of faith in the theatre; it never loses sight of the fact that, as John Holloway wrote in *The Story of the Night*, 'before it is a source of insight, great imaginative literature is a source of power'.[13] Here that power is symbolized by magic happenings, like the transformation of the stuffy Constable; but the real source of that magic, creative energy, is never forgotten. The kind of theatre that Arden and D'Arcy call for in this play is that Peter Brook called Rough Theatre – popular, eclectic, intimate, and pragmatic in its approach:

> . . . putting over something in rough conditions is like a revolution, for anything that comes to hand can be turned into a weapon. The Rough Theatre doesn't pick and choose: if the audience is restive, then it is obviously more important to holler at the trouble makers – or improvise a gag – than to try to preserve the unity of style of the scene. . . . The popular theatre, freed of unity of style, actually speaks a very sophisticated and stylish language: a popular audience usually has no difficulty in accepting inconsistencies of accent and dress, or in darting between mime and dialogue, realism and suggestion.[14]

The definition sums up much of the excitement and freedom of Arden's best work, embodying as it does the sort of spirit found in Pieter Bruegel's painting of *Carnival and Lent.*

The Royal Pardon and the other writings discussed in this chapter so far reflect one aspect of Arden's concern with theatre, that of style. His work also reveals another, equally profound, preoccupation – that of the responsibility of the playwright to society. Perhaps the most detailed, witty and complex exploration of the question can be found in his radio play *The Bagman*, written in 1969 before Arden's trip to India. Arden's political thinking had already begun to change – he resigned from an honorary position on the pacifist paper *Peace News* later that year – and in some ways *The Bagman* is a sort of prophecy of his Indian experiences. Ironically enough, Martin Esslin, then head of BBC Drama and the director of the play, saw it as an exploration of the 'dilemma' of a liberal intellectual artist who feels himself unable to change the society he so accurately portrays. Arden has energetically rejected this view, in his preface to the published edition and in his radio interview with Ronald Hayman. Even without this repeated denial on his part Esslin's view seems rather perverse. One has only to read the play, or, curiously, to hear Esslin's own production, to catch its tone clearly. It is a painfully honest and highly entertaining piece of self-satire.

The central figure is a playwright, 'John Arden', portrayed in the radio production by Alan Dobie with a wicked imitation of Arden's own Yorkshire vowels. It is clear from the beginning that Arden sees 'Arden' as a weak, feeble creature with very little sense of responsibility. We first meet him in search of an evening paper, without which he 'stood alone and felt quite ill'. It is as if the mere knowing about current events can somehow render him valuable; without his *Standard* or *Evening News* he is reduced to asking who he is, what he is for. His answer is not encouraging – if he dies, no-one would notice, life would not change.

He falls asleep, and 'as I slept I dreamed a dream'. The reference to Bunyan is clear, and the contrast is obvious. Bunyan's dream was, of course, *Pilgrim's Progress*, a work which is very sure of itself and what it has to say about society; Bunyan is an active, lively dreamer. 'Arden' says plaintively that 'the dream rose up at me' and throughout the rest of the play he is constantly falling asleep and having dreams within dreams – a situation which conveniently absolves him from taking any responsibility for his own actions at all.

In his dream, he buys from an old woman a bag which proves to be full of tiny people; they form a sort of repertory company for Arden plays: there is a Soldier in a red coat, a Policeman, a King and Queen and a Girl with bright eyes. He wanders with his bag through a world which suggests Toytown rewritten by Kafka; some of the people are rich and fat and dirty; some are starving and oppressed – he sees a man nailed to a tree, crying about freedom. They are all kept in order by a clean, trim, utterly terrifying police force who maintain that 'those who deserve to eat, eat'. The government consists of two ministers, one who supplies entertainment and cosy platitudes, and one who allegedly confronts the people with harsh home truths, but who really exists to provide a stimulating showerbath of Puritanism without involving them in any genuine social change.

'Arden's' little people perform plays in this environment and prove an enormous success; and the central section of the play is taken up with an exploration of the way in which the playwright can be used and exploited by a corrupt society. 'Arden' does not feel in control of his little people; he sets them out on the stage and their performance seems to arise spontaneously; he does not seem to realize, as the ministers do, that 'the whole performance was informed by the fellow's own personality' – in other words, that he does have some choice about his own plays.

We get an account of two of these plays. The first is a 'tragedy' of the kind that Brecht hated. A group of poor people attack the rich, fail, and finally succeed, killing the cruel king and destroying the wicked queen in fine French Revolutionary style; but they are brought down in turn by quarrelling among themselves until their little Republic lies in ruins:

> The conclusion was ominous. Hacked and splintered wooden limbs lay everywhere upon the platform, and of those manikins who were not dead only the most crippled and the weakest seemed to have enough voice to bewail their ill-fortune and to call upon the world for redress. None who watched were able to restrain their tears. The more so because all this time an unseen music had been ringing and clanging, stirring the heart and turning the entrails of all that spellbound auditory . . .

The people thoroughly enjoy the moving spectacle; then, no doubt purged by pity and terror in the best tragic tradition, they go off to watch a public execution. The ministers meanwhile debate what to do with 'Arden'; although his gift might be potentially dangerous, they can see his value. He provides an entertainment which ultimately reinforces the *status quo* by reducing social evils to an emotional experience. As the Popular Minister puts it, 'They know themselves fat because the outlandish men are thin: they suffer now and then in their consciences for this. Either we can help them to forget it, as I do: or else, like this Professor fellow, we can occasionally remind them, let them feel a temporary pang, and their discomfort is assuaged.'

Consequently, they take 'Arden' over; he is to be a playwright for the state, and in return they will give him money, pleasant surroundings, good audiences, a chance to experiment and 'small personal gratifications appropriate to your status'. Ronald Hayman likens these blandishments to those offered to Brecht by the East German government; they are not very different to those given to any writer working for a state-subsidized organization (apart, perhaps, from the 'small personal gratifications', which seems to mean women). 'Arden' enjoys them. He relishes his bag of little people, although he still cannot control them. Eventually, when he receives the ultimate accolade, a Royal Command Performance, he finds that their style has changed; they perform their second play, a bit of glittery titillation reminiscent of *Oh! Calcutta!*; he finds that this too is greatly appreciated as a penetrating analysis of society, and that he is seen as a picturesque rebel against convention. But he is beginning to feel vaguely ashamed. The Ambassador, a gross and powerful man, gets to the root of the matter:

> You set afoot unauthorised imitations of people you should despise and you blow them out like bullfrogs with the imagination of their strength. *At* the same time, however, you reserve to yourself a sharp pin with which you can at your own convenience prick their distended bellies and explode them into nothing. The first part of

1. *Live like Pigs,* London 1958

2. *Serjeant Musgrave's Dance*, London 1959

3. *Serjeant Musgrave's Dance*, London 1965

4. *The Hero Rises Up*, London 1968

5. *The Island of the Mighty*, London 1972

your programme, from my point of view, is abhorrent. From the point of view of the underdog people to whom you address yourself, the second part is likewise. Therefore you are very bold, and a man to be objectively admired; or else you are a hedger and a fencesitter, and a contemptible poltroon.

The last part of the play enables us to pass the final judgement. 'Arden' falls in with a young woman who teaches him, in a fierce parody of the colonial system, about the economic basis of their society. He decides to join with the revolutionaries. The situation is urgent; she urges him to abandon his bag; but, he bleats, he has *paid* for it; then he realises that his gift can be a weapon, and he dedicates his little men to the cause. But they refuse to get involved:

> We are neat and well-considered little people –
> If you bring us into battle
> You bring us only into grief and woe . . .

and the revolution is crushed as 'Arden' wakes up. He finds himself at Highgate Underground, equally convenient for his home in Muswell Hill or the grave of Karl Marx. And he sees the old woman who mocks him:

> You did not find what you expected
> What you found you did not use
> What you saw you did not look at
> When you looked at it you would not choose!

'Arden' finds himself looking at people in a new way; suddenly, the world is divided into fat and thin people. But he still cannot see himself as able to do anything. 'All I can do', he says plaintively, 'is to look at what I see. . . .'

But it is surely plain that 'Arden' is, as his creator puts it, 'reprehensible, cowardly, and not to be imitated'. Arden sees the writer as in full control of his talent. It is essential to choose how this talent will be used; the alternative is not neutrality or objectivity, but exploitation by the ruling power to serve its own ends. It seems, from the degeneration of 'Arden's' plays, that this will inevitably involve a corresponding decline in artistic quality. The writer's gift may be bestowed arbitrarily (although not without cost) but once given it must be used in full consciousness of its implications. Arden's own choice is plain enough. He states in his preface to *The Bagman*:

> I hope I have made clear . . . that I recognise as the enemy the fed man, the clothed man, the sheltered man, whose food, clothes and house are obtained at the expense of the hunger, the nakedness, and the exposure of so many millions of others: and who will allow anything to be *said*, in books or on the stage, so long as the food, clothes and house remain undiminished in his possession.

Thus the responsibility he feels, as a playwright, to the society in which he lives is firmly established. A question which has preoccupied him frequently over the last ten years or so is related to this – namely, the responsibility of society to the playwright; and in particular, the responsibility of that area of society with which the playwright is most closely concerned, the theatre as a whole. The issue crystallized for both Arden and D'Arcy around their dispute with the Royal Shakespeare Company over *The Island of the Mighty* in 1972; but, as *The Bagman* shows, the relationship between the writer and the subsidized theatres was a matter which had worried Arden for some time. In fact, as far back as 1965 the question seemed to be in his mind. In an interview with Albert Hunt, Arden expressed some fairly light-hearted forebodings. 'You get somebody like Lord Chandos on the National Theatre Board and the mind boggles. I wouldn't like to think that the theatre in the next few years was going to be run between the Aldwych and the National rather like the world is run between Moscow and Washington . . .'[15]

By 1972, few theatres apart from the National and the two Royal Shakespeare Company theatres had sufficient financial resources to stage a lengthy and ambitious project by a writer not known for commercial success, and it was the Royal Shakespeare Company which decided to stage the longest and most demanding play (or rather, series of plays) which Arden and D'Arcy had yet written. A bitter dispute ensued. Arden sat in on the first six weeks of rehearsals, while D'Arcy waited for the first run-through in order to bring a fresh eye to the production. When the run-through was staged, about two weeks before the first night, both authors found themselves very unhappy with it; they felt that the play's anti-imperialistic stance had been blurred and distorted, partly by the extensive cuts and partly by the style of the production. They hoped to solve some of the problems with a meeting of everyone concerned; when this did not happen they withdrew their labour and picketed the theatre. At the preview, some of their supporters stopped the play and called for a full discussion; but when Arden offered to speak, a large part of the audience shouted him down. Arden and D'Arcy left the theatre and returned to Ireland, Arden saying as he left 'We will never write for you again'.

The Press, of course, had a field day; there were lurid accounts of the dispute and another controversy over a letter written to the *Times* by Trevor Nunn, Artistic Director of the Royal Shakespeare Company, and David Jones, who directed the play, in which they described the Royal Shakespeare Company as 'a basically left-wing organisation'. Sadly, all the ballyhoo tended to submerge not only the very real merits of the play but also the issues at stake. The important point Arden and D'Arcy wished to make was inscribed on one of the placards on the picket line: 'Playwrights are workers before they are artists.' As workers, they felt that they had the right to strike. The dispute brought home the fact that a playwright has no legal right over the interpretation of his or her play; it was a relative novelty for Arden and D'Arcy to be paid for their attendance at rehearsals and they had no automatic right to resist cuts, business or costumes that they felt to be wrong. They have, subsequently, been active in the Theatre Writers' Union and Arden has expressed the hope that this body will become an effective agent of change in the theatre.[16]

Arden has subsequently dealt with the question in more considered detail in his essay *Playwrights and Play-Writers*, first delivered as a lecture in Australia in 1975. In it he calls for a radical change in current theatrical thinking about the respective roles of writer and director. Just how radical these changes would be can be gauged by the response of the *Sun* – a paper not normally noted for its interest in theatre – to the *Island of the Mighty* dispute.

> WHAT ARROGANCE to inflict his views on people who have paid for an evening's entertainment and who want a chance to judge his play for themselves.
> WHAT ARROGANCE to suppose that a top director and

company are not entitled to their interpretation of a play if it happens to be different from the author's.

Mr. Arden told the audience that he would never write for them again. Fair enough. For whom will he write if not for those who are prepared to pay to support the live theatre?[17]

The headline, BRÀIN STOPS PLAY, suggests that the *Sun* feels – and presumably expects its readers to feel – that the sole authority to interpret a play belongs to the director, while the playwright exists on some kind of disembodied plane out of the way of the real action, coming down to earth, apparently, only to collect his pay. It is interesting that no attempt is made to talk about the rights and wrongs of this particular case, to assess the quality of the play or the production. The director's status is simply taken as read.

In *Playwrights and Play-Writers* Arden explodes this idea. He attacks the 'emasculating elevation' of the director over the playwright, which he sees as arising originally from the inefficiency of nineteenth-century acting companies rather than as a natural development. The current exaltation of the director by bodies such as the Arts Council he sees as politically dangerous. The director's control of both the administrative and artistic functions of an acting company gives him considerable power – power which, Arden feels, is often used to soften or gloss over the more dangerous points of view made by the playwrights with whom he works. Arden also attacks the devaluation of the spoken word which results from the high value placed on the director's skills in non-verbal aspects of theatre. The inevitable result, he feels, is

the international theatre-group, swooping by jumbo-jet

from one cultural function to another all over the world
. . . a non-verbal compost of currently-received physical
images which can mean all things to all men . . .
'Controversy', if aroused at all, is set afoot only by
such classless generalities as naked bodies, cursorily-
motivated violence, and a broad demonstration of
'compassion for the human condition'.[18]

This does less than justice to international theatre
practitioners like Peter Brook, but it is nonetheless
interesting that Brook has worked extensively in recent
years on Shakespeare on the one hand and on ideas, rather
than texts, on the other. One of his most fruitful
associations has been with the poet Ted Hughes, who
would be classified by Arden as a 'playwriter' rather than a
'playwright'. It is a distinction to which he attaches some
importance. A playwriter is anyone – a novelist or poet for
instance – who may wish to express himself or herself,
once in a while, in the form of a play. Such a person may
well need the director to help with stage-craft. But a
playwright is a person who makes plays as a wheelwright
makes wheels; and, ideally, a playwright should have the
ability to translate his or her own play into physical terms.

Arden looks back to a society in which the possibility
existed – to the director-free theatre of Shakespeare and
Jonson. There was certainly an administrative control,
which came from the principal shareholders. But the actual
stage practice sprang from the involvement of the
playwright with the skills and traditions of the company.
Any company would have developed a way of setting out
certain 'stock' scenes – a King receiving an Embassy, say,
or addressing his army. These would follow certain lines
laid down; the individual colour and richness of these
scenes in a particular play would come out of the

playwright's lines and the rhythms they imposed. The appearance of Brachiano's ghost with the skull in *The White Devil*, for instance, might employ some of the same stylized groupings and actions as Hamlet's entry into Ophelia's funeral holding the skull of Yorick; but the scenes are quite different in flavour and impact. A playwright in Arden's sense of the word would draw great strength from the company, if his verbal skill matched his understanding of the resources available to him. Arden adduces the war framework of *Hamlet* as an example of what could be accomplished. Few words are spent on the Fortinbras part of the plot, but good use of the marching troops and warlike demeanour of the Norwegian 'extras' adds another dimension to the play, extending the plot outwards from the simplicities of private revenge into a complex, rewarding study of a whole society.

We are back, in short, to the theatre of Jonson with which this chapter began, and to which Arden looked at the beginning of his career. He is aware that in putting forward this ideal he is calling for a revolution in the theatre; playwrights are not born with these skills and the present theatrical structure does not help them to acquire them. Arden feels that this is as good a reason as any for changing that structure – and this, he points out, will be hard to achieve without political and social revolution too.

4
Matter

. . . We are the iron shield
Screwed tight upon the buried face below:
John Arden sees us: we see him: we know.

(John Arden, *Here I Come*)

In 1968 Arden and D'Arcy wrote a play about Nelson, *The Hero Rises Up*. It was performed at the Roundhouse, a theatre which had strong links with the New Wave of the 50s and latterly with the young underground, and did not go on without a certain amount of struggle between the playwrights and their management, the Institute for Contemporary Arts. In 1970 Terence Rattigan, the strongest and most enduring pillar of the established theatre throughout all the changes of the preceding decade, wrote a play about Nelson, *A Bequest to the Nation*; it was performed at the Haymarket, one of London's largest and most beautiful commercial theatres. To look at these plays side by side is to see the debate about theatre initiated at

78

the Royal Court come to energetic life; and to see in sharp relief the specifically political qualities of Arden's and D'Arcy's imagination.

A Bequest to the Nation is a play about the private Nelson. It centres on one question; why did Nelson cling to the ageing and not always sober Lady Hamilton and reject his wife with such hatred? This is the problem Nelson tries to articulate to Hardy the night before he goes off to Trafalgar. He manages to convey the contrast between the sexuality of the one and the intolerable forgiveness of the other before walking off into history, leaving onstage the dinner silver he has arranged in the shape of his battle-plan of Trafalgar, over which, in the final scene, the two women achieve some sort of reconciliation.

For Rattigan, then, the most interesting part of his hero is his clay feet. The fact that he *is* a hero is taken for granted; we never see him in action and we never see the results of that action for society as a whole; the play is set in private rooms in rich men's houses; the working people of England are represented by one hero-worshipping servant-girl. It is the business of the actors to identify with their characters – Zoe Caldwell put on weight specially to play Lady Hamilton – not to judge them.

Arden and D'Arcy are concerned not with one man but with, as Brecht put it, 'man as the sum total of all human relations'.[1] They begin their play by asking us to think about the nature of heroism: 'To understand what makes a hero is to understand, perhaps, how we in our own society may be able to make one for ourselves – or even become one – who knows?' Their chosen setting and style is as colourful and unrealistic as a circus or a toy theatre; it never ceases to remind us that we are watching a play and that we can judge the events in it for ourselves. They show us not only Nelson's wealthy social circle but the people

affected by his actions; for instance, a chorus of sailors
sing about Nelson's capture of the Neapolitan
revolutionary, Caracciolo. The tune is a jolly sea-shanty;
but they suit the actions to the increasingly ironic words:

> We caught the chief of all the gang
> Sing ho for liberty
> And we beat him down with many a bang
> We meant to make him free.

> We tied his arms with a length of twine
> Sing ho for liberty
> And we dragged him up at the end of a line
> That's how we made him free.

It is sung in the presence of the King and Queen of Naples
and Lady Hamilton, all of them baying frenetically for
blood. Nelson's great love affair is thus seen sharply in a
political context. And Nelson's stepson Nisbet relates the
sick society of Naples to conditions in England:

> For had they all known who he was –
> Being ragged dirty British skin-and-bone –
> It is just possible they would have cried
> For a bold Caracciolo of their own.

Nelson himself makes his first dynamic entrance jumping
through a paper screen like a clown through a hoop; he
also outlines the naval strategy that gave him his heroic
status: 'I was the first naval commander who understood –
and put into practice – the theory of the entire and total
destruction of the enemy fleet, at whatever cost to my
own.' We are never, in short, permitted to identify with
him or offer him our unqualified admiration.

We are not allowed to despise him either. Although the overt theatricality of the play works as an alienation device, it has another function. The use of songs and circus tricks, jokes, dances, fireworks and the concluding tableau with Nelson going up to heaven in a mermaid-spangled chariot also serve to charge it with a tremendous energy which both reflects and celebrates that of the central figure. The final judgement is not upon one man but on a society that has no better use for his extraordinary qualities but to set him killing on its behalf.

Arden and D'Arcy describe the tension between Nelson and the world that shaped him in terms of an old struggle between the Celtic values of this country and those of its Roman and English conquerors. In a preface to the play almost as quirky and entertaining as the play itself, they talk about their own struggles with the Institute of Contemporary Arts as a reflection of that same conflict. The terminology they use is – although a highly personal one – extremely useful in discussing their work, or that of Arden alone. They think of the Celtic virtues as 'curvilinear', rather like the plastic virtues of their art, embodied in the Book of Kells – passionate, wayward, devious, intuitive, energetic – as opposed to the Roman 'rectilinear' virtues – order, 'doing things properly', efficiency, organization (the trains run on time). To think of Arden as an exponent of the curvilinear is perhaps to find a consistency of approach to his work before and after the change in his political outlook.

The year before *The Bagman*, 1968, marked the beginning of that change. It was also a watershed year for British theatre. In looking at Arden as a political playwright it is, therefore, important to examine his work on both sides of that dividing line. It is not simply that the plays are different, but the whole theatrical context in which they took place also underwent a startling metamorphosis of its own.

The Royal Court of the 50s was not really a political theatre. Many (not all) of the writers it championed would have described themselves as socialists, or at least opposed to the conduct of the Conservative government, especially in foreign affairs such as the Suez crisis. Many of them wrote about social classes which their immediate predecessors had not bothered to represent onstage, except as caricatures. But this, as John Whiting pointed out in an energetic attack entitled, polemically, *At Ease in a Bright Red Tie*, did not constitute political theatre:

> Their concern with humanist values is admirable, but it is so often expressed merely by a sort of kindness . . . their sympathy for minorities and the under-privileged is apt to become sentimental, and end up with no more than the handing round of tea and buns in St. Pancras Town Hall . . . with their failure to come to grips with the political philosophy they profess, and working in a style which is deteriorating into the most trivial reporting of fact, these writers can hardly expect the revolution to continue.[2]

Certainly few of the Court group offered a political analysis of the events they depicted with such vivid realism. Whiting's criticism is not altogether fair, however, in that it seems to be assuming an intention that was by no means present among the whole group. They were a very mixed bunch; of the four major figures whose work is still frequently seen and discussed – Osborne, Pinter, Arden and Wesker – only the last two could really be described as political writers at all. Osborne's sympathies have always been clear enough: once vociferously Left, he is now vociferously Right; but his work is concerned with feelings rather than ideas, with invective rather than analysis; his special energies spring from sources other than politics. Pinter's plays are in no sense political (although his characters seem to have risen a little on the social scale as time goes on). Wesker's commitment to socialism and his own brand of socialist realism remains unchanged. Only Arden has moved towards a more firmly committed left-wing stance. But of all the new writers of the 50s, Arden had, perhaps, the strongest political imagination.

Arden has always portrayed man in society rather than man in the drawing room. He has perhaps the most sharply developed historical sense of all his contemporaries. While plays like *Luther* and *A Man for All Seasons* teach us something about Luther and More, they tell us little about the society that shaped them; they are essentially costume pieces of high quality. With Arden we are always sharply aware of what it was like to be alive at a certain time, what people wore, what they ate, how they saw the universe, how they talked. His historical plays often had conscious parallels in contemporary politics. *Serjeant Musgrave's Dance* was inspired by an incident in Cyprus and *Armstrong's Last Goodnight* by the role of the United Nations in the Congo.

While his talent for coping with a broad social canvas has always been appreciated, Arden's essentially socialist position has not. One of the critical clichés of the 50s was 'you never know where he stands'. John Russell Taylor describes his intelligent and muscular verse in glowing terms in his introduction to three of the plays, but adds 'there is a determined refusal to take sides on a number of questions where almost any audience would conventionally be inclined to suppose that side-taking was imperative'[3], and even worries that the relative like-

ability of Krank in *The Waters of Babylon* might be
misinterpreted as pro-Nazi if Arden did not make his
condemnation plain. Arden's neutrality became taken for
granted, to the point where Edwin Morgan, discussing
Armstrong's Last Goodnight, could reduce it to a sort of
critical shorthand: 'This is an Arden play! Sympathy never
develops very far.'[4]

This response really depends upon one assumption –
that 'sympathy' must always be given to a particular
character, that we should look, in the Stanislavski
tradition, for a figure with whom we can identify. Any
attempt to do this in an Arden play inevitably leads to
frustration (and, perhaps, to use his own phrase, a desire
that he would 'do things properly' in an orderly, rectilinear
manner). But there is another and more rewarding way of
looking at the plays, which is to observe the *action*, and to
ask, 'Need it have happened like that?' A definite
perspective immediately reveals itself. In, for instance,
Live Like Pigs, we cannot take sides in the punch-up
between the gipsy-like Sawneys and the stuffy Jacksons.
But we can understand why it takes place. Arden vividly
conveys the dreary quality of life on the housing estate on
which families are flung together willy-nilly by hectoring
authorities, to whom the Sawneys react with violence and
the Jacksons with genteel complaint. 'Of course it's a long
way from the shops and there's only the one public. But
my husband he reckons that's a good thing.' Similarly *The
Waters of Babylon* depicts a galaxy of characters towards
whom our feelings are very complex. But the play, which
takes its title from a psalm about the bitterness and
injustice of exile, shows a whole society which erodes the
richness of immigrant cultures and offers only a cheap and
flashy materialism in their place. We are not invited to
extend sympathy; we are asked to place our indignation.

Catherine Itzin sees the early refusal to recognize Arden's political commitment as an almost wilful attempt to misunderstand his style in order to ignore his world view: 'The initial hostility and lack of comprehension was a response (however subconscious) to the radical and disturbing political implications of the plays.'[5] Wilful or not, such a response became less and less possible as the 60s gave way to the 70s. And after 1968, Arden was not alone in his political stance.

This was the year in which the Soviet Union invaded Czechoslovakia; the year of the revolt by students and workers in Paris; the year of the Tet offensive in Vietnam; the year Civil Rights marchers in Derry were brutally beaten up. It was also the year in which Parliament ended censorship in the theatre and the beginning of what came to be seen as a second wave of new writers like Howard Brenton, David Hare, Trevor Griffiths and David Edgar. Like their 1956 predecessors, they were socialist in outlook; but unlike them, they were committed to socialism *as writers*, not just in their personal lives. Other more established writers, Edward Bond, for example, and John McGrath, began to move over the next decade towards a more consciously developed political analysis in their work; Bond's plays of the later 70s, for instance, not only looked at society but also suggested ways of changing it: 'I'm now going on', he wrote in 1977, 'to a series of plays which I will call "answer plays", in which I would like to say: I have stated the problems as clearly as I can – now let's try and look at what answers are applicable.'[6]

The difference between 1968 and 1956 was not solely a matter of the relative commitment of major writers. The theatre of the 50s remained, despite attempts by Arnold Wesker, Joan Littlewood and others to develop a truly popular theatre, firmly London-based and middle-class in its appeal. The first avowedly socialist theatre of the 60s was Roland Muldoon's group CAST, formed in 1965; after 1968 a wgole series of radical companies were formed – Agit Prop Street Players, Red Ladder, followed in the 70s by still others – Belt and Braces, Hull Truck, Monstrous Regiment. They both nourished the new writers and were nourished by them; John McGrath set up 7.84, Hare and Brenton Portable Theatre. They played not only established venues but also in places that were not theatres in any accepted sense, in pubs and clubs and local halls, to people who had rejected conventional theatre or had had no opportunity to see it.

The theatrical context in which Arden found himself after the Indian visit (which led him to say that he would in future view whatever he wrote through the eyes of an Indian revolutionary)[7] was therefore very different from that in which he had begun to write. And Arden and D'Arcy had their own impact upon the changes. The new groups and new writers used a variety of styles to make themselves clear. Trevor Griffiths, for instance, was largely committed to naturalism because he felt that the unfamiliar ideas he was expressing might be more easily accepted in a familiar form; 7.84 used the traditions of naturalism, although rather more freely, in the early years. Their performance of Arden and D'Arcy's *The Ballygombeen Bequest*, however, had a marked effect on their style and they were subsequently to use the techniques of the music hall, the cartoon, the ceilidh and the circus with considerable success.

India revealed in clear focus a tension which can be seen at work in most of the later plays of Arden and D'Arcy – that between revolution and reform. The relationship between the Marxist-Leninist Naxalites and the non-violent Ghandians illuminated much of their thinking about Ireland. Arden has, since that visit, concentrated to a very great extent upon the question of Ireland. This has meant that most of his plays since 1969 have been written with D'Arcy, herself Irish; and it also makes him a unique figure in British theatre. Some of Britain's leading political dramatists have not written about Ireland at all – Bond, for example. Others have dealt with the subject only once or twice. Their experiences while doing so may explain this fact: Brenton, Hare, Edgar, Tony Bicat, Brian Clark, Francis Fuchs and Snoo Wilson constructed a show called *England's Ireland* in 1972, which more than fifty theatres refused to handle. Caryl Churchill's play about the Diplock Courts, *The Legion Hall Bombing*, was only transmitted by the BBC in 1978 after alterations which led her to ask for her name to be removed from the credits. The 1981 controversy about Brenton's play *The Romans in Britain* may arise as much from what it has to say about Ireland as from its scenes of homosexual rape.

Arden has had his own struggles; when, for instance, he was offered a commission by the BBC in 1971 and suggested the life of the Irish revolutionary leader Connolly as a possible subject, he was told that 'passions' in Northern Ireland might be 'inflamed'. He has complained that some of his work with D'Arcy has been rejected in favour of what is described as 'genuine Arden work', and that this is essentially a way of censoring, indirectly, his Irish material. Yet he continues to treat the choice of Irish subject matter as the only responsible one for a practising playwright. An article in the *New Statesman* in 1979 traced the impact of the Protestant Reformation on English literature to the present day; Arden feels that from Spenser and John Bale onwards certain prejudices have been present but never voiced, that 'we find always recurrent the same strange vein of obsessed distressed uncomprehending hostility to Irish habits of life and their political embodiment'.[8] His own task as a writer is to help readers and audiences to come to terms with this 'infected heritage' and to see the Irish situation with the clear sight with which many of them could approach the political problems of a foreign land.

In looking at the later plays of Arden (and, in most cases, D'Arcy) one is, as it were, entering a complex and continuing debate. It is possible with a writer like Bond to examine the nature of his political ideas without reference to a specific situation. The 'answer' plays are set in remote areas, historically and geographically; *The Bundle*, for instance, is set in an Asian location and the period is simply 'this century'. With Arden, however, we are forced to talk in highly specific terms, about real places and people; his work is a mosaic of actual events and experiences as well as more general reflections; and the staging of the most recent plays written with D'Arcy has sometimes constituted in itself a political act. Of the four major plays performed in England since *The Island of the Mighty* – *The Ballygombeen Bequest*, *The Non-Stop Connolly Show*, *Vandaleur's Folly* and *Pearl* (Arden's only Irish play, at present, to have been written without D'Arcy) – this is especially true of the two former, also staged in Ireland. This chapter will concentrate upon them, because they illuminate Arden's political thinking by their context as well as their content.

The Ballygombeen Bequest looks at the triangular relationship between Northern Ireland, England, and the Irish Republic, and at the relationship between all three parties and socialism; and it does so by concentrating on a particular local issue. 1971 saw a tourist boom around Galway and the land suddenly became very attractive to big hotel chains. As it rocketed in value certain local groups became very vulnerable – notably farmers, who needed arable land but found that the Land Commission favoured the hoteliers, and tenants whose rights were not completely secure. Lacking other help many turned to the IRA. Bulldozers were blown up and guns fired at the police.

Meanwhile, Arden was commissioned by a London theatre to write a play about 'Ulster'. Aware, through the Galway situation, that the problems of North and South were intrinsically linked, Arden and D'Arcy began *The Ballygombeen Bequest*; when it was finished the play was rejected on the grounds that 'it was, like most litigation, only of interest to the litigants'.[9] It seemed that scenes showing the torture by British troops of an IRA man were acceptable; but an analysis of the *economic* reasons for their presence was not. Consequently it was a Belfast teacher training college that first staged the play in the Falls Road – a courageous act on their part and one which suggests that Arden's idea of the theatre as a place for political exploration as well as entertainment is shared at least by people actually living in a political situation of agonizing complexity.

Subsequently, the play was performed at the Edinburgh Festival and the Bush Theatre in London by the 7.84 Company. In Edinburgh a duplicated sheet was issued giving details about a specific case; Arden and D'Arcy (who had not written it) were promptly sued for libel and slander. The case was *sub judice* from 1973 to 1977 and the play could not be performed. When it finally came up before Judge Melford Stevenson it provided an interesting clash of styles: the prosecution's main point was that the landlord *in the play* got his tenant drunk in order to make him sign away his rights; Arden and D'Arcy wanted the play to be seen as a piece of fictional allegory and

attempted to discuss the history of the English presence in
Ireland. They finally settled out of court, but not before
the judge had uttered a verdict on the play in the tradition
of the early *Musgrave* notices: 'It is unfortunate that the
jury should have to read this turgid piece of prose.' (*sic*)[10]
Once again, the debate seemed to be not whether the play
was a bad one, but whether it was a play at all.

It was certainly a political act, and reflected a tendency
in fringe theatre generally to erode the boundaries between
art and life. Sandy Craig traces this to the influence of the
artist Jean-Jacques Lebel whose ideas led to the
'happenings' of the 60s and later to more directly political
acts of theatre:

> Lebel's practice was the theatrical equivalent of the
> international situationists' political theory of the
> spectacle of every day life, which, in a revision of Marx,
> stated that the focus of capitalist domination was at the
> point of consumption, not the point of production. The
> influence of Lebel and the international situationists
> was widespread – from performance art groups and
> writers like Howard Brenton and Snoo Wilson to more
> authentic Marxists like John McGrath.[11]

Arden's and D'Arcy's attendance at the first London
performance of *The Ballygombeen Bequest* instead of the
first night of *The Island of the Mighty* was also a political
statement about theatre. They chose to commit themselves
to the play which, they felt, contained the greater potential
for bringing about social change, rather than to the play
with the larger and more prestigious audience. As Arden
wrote in 1972, the concept of a National Theatre was an
anomaly in a divided nation; it was necessary to decide

which 'nation' one was writing for. 'It is probable that we will find ourselves performing for smaller and smaller audiences in more and more smaller halls . . . and the members of the audiences will want plays that express in some way their own consciousness of being cheated, exploited and deprived.'[12]

However, *The Ballygombeen Bequest* is, *pace* Judge Melford Stevenson, also a play, and a very entertaining and lucid one. Its images are sharply economical; for instance, as soon as the villainous Lieutenant-Colonel Hollidey-Cheype has bounded onstage and wondered what to do in post-war England, a letter is handed to him by the stage manager containing the details of the estate bequeathed to him in Ireland. It is funny, in its very obvious theatricality – but it also makes a political point, suggesting by its magical promptness the potential for exploitation in the Irish Republic. As Hollidey-Cheype discovers in seconds from his helpful solicitor, there are no post-war shortages and no Labour Government to cramp his style: 'The bishops sit on that pot: oh, very firm posteriors the bishops have over there . . . no rationing . . . you can buy a ham in the west of Ireland the size of a bishop's buttock.' The way is open for the rich to get richer, and money smooths the relations between England and the Republic – at whose expense is soon made clear. The talent of both Arden and D'Arcy for suggesting a whole way of life in a few phrases is here in full force; Hollidey-Cheype's two properties are described so vividly that they constantly keep before us the class war in Ireland; the flashy jerry-built bungalow with its poor plumbing and disruptive local builders on the make, fetching huge sums of money from well-off holiday-makers, contrasts sharply with the smoke and mice and earth closet of the O'Learys' cottage with its picturesque thatch that lets in the rain.

John Arden

In 1956, the O'Learys are still being exploited. The Conservatives are in power in England and Hollidey-Cheype is using the O'Learys to make money for him in Ireland. He describes the new relationship between the North of Ireland and the South:

> It is not like that, these days, in the West –
> The bitter glue of Irish politics
> In that soft climate now no longer sticks.
> A Unionist, an Orangeman indeed
> Is seen there as the kind of man they need.
> The curdled thunder of his furious drum
> He modifies into the industrious hum
> Of calculating machines. . . .

England and both sides of Ireland are neatly sewn up into a capitalist package; the IRA are proscribed on both sides of the border. Fianna Fail, the Irish ruling party, is represented by the corrupt builder, Hagan. There is nothing and no-one strong enough to prevent Hollidey-Cheype from tying the wretched Seamus O'Leary into legal knots.

So far, we have a picture of one small part of the world. Arden and D'Arcy now widen the context and survey the class war from the 50s to the years of Vietnam:

> From nineteen fifty-seven
> To nineteen sixty-eight
> The fat men of the fat-half world
> Had food on every plate.
> The lean men of the naked world
> Grew leaner every day
> And if they put their faces up

> Their teeth were kicked away:
> And if they dared to link their arms
> Or spread their shoulders wide
> Such furious dogs were set on them
> They bled both back and side.

In other words, the Third World has begun to emerge as a political force, but not yet a political power. The situation is mirrored in Ballygombeen. Seamus is dead, helped to the grave by the attempt to evict him; the fight is now in the hands of his son Padraic; like the lean men the world over he is able to articulate his anger – he has learned his Marxism during a Manchester building strike – but he cannot yet fight effectively. He tragically underestimates the forces working against him. Hollidey-Cheype is not alone; he has contacts in British Intelligence and fluently explains to them why the efforts of an Irish tenant to stop the eviction of his family are closely related to the troubles north of the Border. Padraic is watched not only by a British agent (in comic disguise as a film producer) but also by one from Dublin Castle. As his sister Siobahn puts it, both North and South are governed by the Man with the Long Purse. Meanwhile, Padraic's final hope, the Official IRA, tell him that the Ballygombeen affair is 'peripheral'. So the way is open for the ubiquitous Hagan, who offer to blow up the bungalow; he knows that the land will then be seen as 'marked' by the IRA and sold off cheap. But he is also determined that Padraic will not survive; he can cope with the IRA but not with an avowed Marxist. So he betrays Padraic to British Intelligence and Dublin Special Branch, who set a trap for him: driving north of the border to sell ponies in Hagan's van, Padraic is arrested and dies under torture. His body is dumped near the border, carefully doctored to look like a victim of IRA internecine strife.

Arden and D'Arcy make it clear that the real enemy of people like the O'Learys is capitalism. While the murder of Padraic is shown in violent detail, the troops are not seen as monsters. 'You find me a good job in England, boy', says one of them, 'I tell you I'd never have set foot.' They are part of a machine created on both sides of the Irish sea to serve capitalist interests; the radio broadcast in which the death of Padraic is announced also contains a comment by the Taoiseach, Mr Lynch, on the detrimental effect of 'illegal organizations' on foreign investment.

The play does not, however, end here. If Arden and D'Arcy were writing a naturalistic play, they would have had to close on a tragic note; however, their chosen style permits an ending full of gaiety and also of challenge. With the end of the O'Learys, the capitalist alliance between Hagan and Hollidey-Cheype dissolves into its usual state of ruthless competition. As they squabble over the price of the bungalow, the ghost of Padraic engineers a custard pie fight of epic proportions, and sings us a song with the timely reminder 'There are more of us than them'. He may be dead, but the real battle is still going on and its ultimate solution is in the hands of the audience.

The Ballygombeen Bequest presents a clear Marxist analysis of the Irish situation. That is not its only argument, however; the quality of the play also speaks. It contains stunningly theatrical images: the killing of Padraic, naked in a darkness lit by one dazzling lamp, is hard to forget. There are music hall routines, such as the display of stage Irishry to which the mocking O'Learys treat Hollidey-Cheype on his first visit; there are sharply satirical songs. The play is constructed so that it can be well performed by a small group with few resources – in itself a political statement about the people it is written for. It may discuss an issue which is painful, but in itself it affords the audience an opportunity for Brecht's ideal of 'a cheerful and militant learning'.[13]

The Ballygombeen Bequest was a rarity in English political theatre in its plain statement of the desirability of a socialist republic in Ireland. *The Non-Stop Connolly Show* was an even greater rarity in that it presented the historical process which underlies that triangular relationship between England and the two parts of Ireland. Its function differed slightly in each country. In Ireland it celebrated a Republican hero and made it clear that Connolly's nationalist and socialist virtues were still necessary. In England it stressed the fact that the reluctance of the British Left to come to terms with the Irish struggle for independence had led to bloodshed and was still doing so; and it attempted to dispense with some of the ignorance that gave rise to that reluctance in the first place.

D'Arcy and Arden knew, in theatrical terms, what they were letting themselves in for. They stated one of their main problems in a little rhyme:

> My name it is James Connolly
> I neither smoke nor drink.
> Come to the theatre for twenty-six hours
> And watch me sit and think.[14]

Although Connolly's last revolutionary days were dramatic enough for any playwright, his life as a whole was blamelessly respectable; he wrote, he worked hard, he chaired committees and made speeches. This was not the sort of material that was likely to attract critical sympathy. The circumstances of the first performance made this even less likely. The cycle was staged in 1975, at Easter, in Dublin's Liberty Hall which is now the headquarters of the

Irish Transport and General Workers' Union but in 1916 was the administrative centre of Connolly's own Citizen Army, from which he marched on Easter Monday to the Post Office. The cast consisted of Irish and English actors, students, trades unionists, children of the Fianna and interested people like Paddy Marsh, a lecturer at University College, Dublin, who wrote an account of rehearsals for *Theatre Quarterly*. It was rehearsed over three months and the authors struggled to establish a co-operative method of production, although, as with Kirbymoorside, they were not always successful. The first performance ran from Easter Saturday to Sunday without a break; afterwards there were shorter versions presented on both sides of the Irish border and a series of rehearsed readings, using different actors, at the Almost Free in London in 1976.

It was the first performance which really captured the spirit of the piece, and which, inevitably, attracted the most critical flak:

> The trade union boys seemed to consider it as a valid medium for worker education, which is all very well, but the audience were about eighty-five per cent middle class students and the trade union types visible were of the white liberal variety. . . . As theatre it was unbelievably inept. The non-participating cast was in full view a good deal of the time, nose-picking, nail-biting, yawning. . . . When the lead hasn't had time to learn his lines and has to read the stuff, there's no way in which the audience can find it believable. . . . the cast raced through their lines and was audible only in snatches due to the MGM style background music which drowned out many of the key speeches. In the last play there was a neo-mythical sequence with boy scouts as

birds and Arden with script in hand was blocking it onstage like a bad school play. It certainly wasn't theatre, and the sheer pedantry managed to make deeply moving events into stultifying boredom. . . . Propaganda, to be effective, must have some basis in fact and must also rely on impact, not pedantry.[15]

This passage is typical in its hostility not only to the play but to the concept behind it. It is fair enough to complain on the grounds of inaudibility or bad sound balance; it may even be fair to assert that a play about a proletarian hero is not doing its job if the audience it attracts is primarily middle class – although one is on shakier ground here; it is tempting to ask how the class of each member of the audience revealed itself (dress? accent? fingernails?). What is less defensible is the use of terms which invite a hostile response from us without giving any real grounds for criticism – the word 'boy scout' for example, inevitably conjures up in English minds a sort of bare-kneed earnestness that is the stuff of farce; the Fianna – the scouts of the Republican movement founded by Countess Marcievicz – participated because their role in the Easter Rising had been a considerable one, and they took it seriously. Similarly the assertion that 'propaganda must have some basis in fact' seems to be implying that the play gets its facts wrong; but this is not substantiated. What finally betrays the basis of this critic's hostility is, however, the word 'stuff'. We are once again faced with the old debate about what constitutes a play, and in this case, a play seems to be defined as something an audience can find 'believable'. A play in which the leading actor reads from a script and the cast can be seen 'out of character' cannot, therefore, be a play. It erodes the distinction between actor and audience; the audience do

97

not sit quietly believing in the illusion before them, passive recipients of a manufactured product. But to discuss this particular play in these terms is to ignore its very *raison-d'être*.

Connolly was a revolutionary socialist; his world view was based on the assumption that 'the history of all existing society is the history of class struggles'.[16] Translated into dramatic terms, this leads to a shift of focus. The naturalistic theatre was essentially bourgeois – that is, it centred upon the individual. A Marxist theatre needs to place the focus upon the whole of the historical process; thus the story of Connolly from Connolly's own perspective needed to show the class struggle throughout the Western world, as well as his part in that struggle. It also needed to pay close attention to the ideas current in that world as well as the events shaped by them. While writing *The Ballygombeen Bequest*, Arden and D'Arcy joined the Official Sinn Fein, at that time reorganizing itself upon socialist lines after splitting with the Provisional wing. It taught them a great deal about the processes of political organization, and led them to the conclusion that the Connolly play would have to show not only the obviously dramatic aspects of his life but the debate and organization which led to them. It was a responsible, adult decision which prevented the Connolly story from acquiring a false and shallow glamour. It meant, however, that the play would demand from its audience both attention and dedication.

Perhaps the most useful analogy with the Connolly plays is that of the medieval miracle cycles. I have already discussed some of the assumptions implicit in the language of these plays; it may be worth pursuing the question further, for the *Guardian* passage just quoted suggests that most critics still operate from bourgeois positions. The medieval attitude may be a more useful one to take in judging *The Non-Stop Connolly Show*. For in the plays which showed the Creation and Fall, the Life of Christ and the Last Judgement, the medieval guilds looked at life *sub specie aeternitatis*; individual feelings might be explored, but they are not the *point* of the plays. They were designed to demonstrate and celebrate the relationship between God and his people, as shown in history; they taught the faithful and also expressed the world view that they already shared.

The audience for *The Non-Stop Connolly Show* was not so united in its beliefs as a medieval one. D'Arcy and Arden have vividly outlined the problems of dealing with the life of a Republican Socialist in a country where one may be a republican but not a socialist, or vice versa, and where even those who share the twin aspects of Connolly's faith are split into factions. There were many local difficulties; a wave of strikes created havoc in Liberty Hall. There was also a widespread acknowledgement, however, even by parties who did not agree with points made in the plays, that a major work about Connolly was an important event and must be done. To watch it or take part was to become part of a political statement – not necessarily the Marxist position of the play itself, but a statement which proclaims the need and the right to explore that position. The cycle may have had flaws and the production may have had problems, but the sheer scale and audacity of the concept should not go unacknowledged.

A study of Connolly as a historical phenomenon rather than simply as an individual demands a canvas of vast proportions. D'Arcy and Arden found in him a unique combination of revolutionary qualities: he was one of the few socialist leaders of his time of working-class origin; he was an internationalist, which led to his work in many countries and to his often lonely opposition to the First World War, an opposition which led to his part in the Easter Rising; he was continuously involved in trade union activities, also on an international scale. This meant that they would be dealing onstage with the history of half the world between Connolly's boyhood in the 1860s and the Rising and its aftermath. It meant, too, that they would have to depict a conflict which engrossed Connolly for most of his life and which their involvement in Irish politics had convinced them was still going on – the conflict between revolution and reform. The conflict has many aspects: D'Arcy and Arden see it behind the complex relationship between nationalism and socialism in Ireland and in many other small nations struggling for independence since the map of the world began to change in 1914; they see it too in the failure of the British Left to cope with Ireland and its refusal to acknowledge England's imperialistic role there.

In preparing the plays they found that they covered an entire room with maps and charts. To attempt to analyze the whole cycle is to run into the same problem. Even a meaningful summary of the events it narrates would run into many pages, and a survey of its many styles, from naturalism to music hall, puppets to debate, would be a huge task. The best way, perhaps, to give some idea of the political imagination at work in it is to look at the two key figures – the Protagonist, Connolly, and the Antagonist, Grabitall.

Grabitall, whose name was taken from some American political cartoons of the 1930s, is a composite figure representing capitalism in various guises. He stalks through the whole cycle. Sometimes he is a kind of Demon King; he introduces the play along with Connolly's mother, who tells him 'proud demon, avaunt!' in pantomime tradition. Sometimes he resembles the Vice of medieval plays – there is a nice literary in-joke which links him to one of the Vice's descendants, Richard III, in a stage direction reading 'Enter Grabitall between two bishops'. Sometimes, he is a real person; throughout the last two plays he is William Martin Murphy, who controlled the press, the transport, the employers and occasionally even the police of Dublin. It is important to understand his role in order to understand the premises on which the whole cycle is based. D'Arcy and Arden have no intention of showing Connolly's opponents as characters, with specific and personal motives for their political behaviour. This is not because they believe individual capitalists are wholly evil, or individual socialists wholly good, but because, like medieval craftsmen, they do not see the Vice as the moral centre of the story. They are not primarily concerned with the debate between socialism and capitalism, but with the way in which republican socialism works in history. Bunyan used the same technique, as Arden's essay on O'Casey shows; the figures encountered by an ordinary Christian attempting to lead a holy life increase in subtlety as they increase in moral sophistication – the real agents of the devil, like Apollyon, are drawn in crude colours, while the everyday problems like Mr Worldly Wiseman are both detailed and delicate. Not that Grabitall should be regarded lightly; on the contrary, this single figure, adapting to every change in the wind, emphasizes the eternal and complex nature of the socialist struggle, and the War Demons in his wake make it clear that the power of capitalism is a force far greater than the sum of its individual adherents.

While Grabitall is Protean, Connolly is consistent. D'Arcy has defined his role in the plays as that of the 'little tailor' of legend who overcame enemies far greater than himself, and this function has many different aspects. One of these is to show through his own background exactly what the evil he is fighting is like; we are made sharply aware of the nature of poverty in scenes like the one in which he has to dig ditches in his slippers because his boots have rotted away – a scene which is not played for pathos, but concentrates on the simple physical details of the problem and shows him making rough and ready repairs with a piece of string. Perhaps the most poignant line in the whole cycle is his father's outburst when, crippled by an accident at work, he is given a job by the council as a lavatory cleaner: 'Begod, 'tis not a job – 'tis a bloody *function* they have given me' which speaks volumes about the relationship between the worker and the value of his labour.

Connolly is also used to present complex arguments which are made clear to us because they are filtered through his own developing understanding. This growth also humanizes him vividly; although he is shown as the product of social and economic forces, he is by no means bloodless or dull. D'Arcy and Arden share with the medieval writers a conviction that, given one basic truth about existence, there is no part of life which it does not touch. Thus Connolly's growing love for his wife Lillie is presented as a political as well as an emotional issue. Realizing that they have been brought up as Protestant and Catholic he makes a simultaneous leap on two fronts. He has been listening to a socialist agitator speaking against Gladstone's Home Rule policy on the grounds that it is simply another way of dividing the working class and ensuring that they never have real power; suddenly he understands that the qualms he feels about marrying someone of a different religion are just another instance of the divide-and-rule policy at work; he gives a cry of 'at last today I know now who I am' as the political and personal conflicts in his life appear in clear focus, ready to be fought and beaten.

Throughout the plays, Connolly is constantly involved in the conflict between nationalism and socialism, revolution and reform. Sometimes the debate is overt; a scene in Part Three shows him coping with questions from nationalists who want to cling on to their own property, unionists who see republicanism as a red herring, Fabians who want slow changes, socialists who insist that his call for revolution is premature. Sometimes it is presented through satire – Maud Gonne and Yeats ('Willie') lapse into middle-class patronage and nationalist whimsy:

MAUD GONNE: I saw Eire the goddess and she wore a robe of green.
CONNOLLY: And I saw a large element of a large class of the ragged riff-raff of Dublin. . . .

Sometimes it is seen through action: Part Three shows the reactions of several parties to the Boer War. At first it is an undignified scuffle between a rantingly self-righteous Boer and gold-hungry Englishmen, who conduct a toilet-roll battle over the head of a very small native bearer. Then it develops: Grabitall and various foreign arms merchants egg the participants on; the Liberal and Labour parties cannot agree and hurl insults at each other. Connolly's response is to condemn the British oppression of the Boers and to declare that 'England's difficulty should be Ireland's opportunity'. He is promptly rapped over the knuckles by Keir Hardie for his opposition to the British Army, although Hardie makes it quite clear that he will only support the aspirations of the Irish Republican

Socialist Party if they happen to coincide with those of the Labour Party in Westminster. This means that he will support Redmond's Irish Parliamentary Party instead. His decision sets off a happy little dance by Grabitall and his cronies, who see their interests as protected.

As the cycle progresses the struggle grows more intense. We see the violence with which the Dublin General Strike is beaten down on Bloody Sunday – as D'Arcy and Arden mordantly point out, not the first day to be so named, nor the last. Part Five ends with Connolly's despair as the British trades unions refuse their support – they do not want outright revolution, or what they call 'irresponsible syndicalism' – and yet the people of Dublin are starving and a slow process of reform will not help them. Then the world erupts into war. We see shady deals between governments and the unions – Asquith promising nationalization in return for a strike-free war. We see the socialist dissenters of Europe – Rosa Luxemburg, Liebknecht, Jaurès – gradually silenced. Against this background Connolly makes his decision to join with Padraig Pearse in the Easter Rising.

He is not shown as wholly right; D'Arcy and Arden use the legend of King Conaire and an extensive dream sequence to make it plain that his choice was in part an emotional one. Like Conaire, Connolly breaks certain prohibitions: he collaborates with people not in full sympathy with his aims, he becomes dependent on imperialist Germany for help, he ignores the Ulster trades unions, he has not rooted his revolution solidly in the working class. And, as history shows, his rebellion failed.

It is pointed out to us, however, that his failure was not the only one. As the rebels are shot one by one, the British trades unions protest about the brutality but simultaneously reject the idea of an independent and socialist Ireland. Lenin speaks his own epitaph on the Rising: 'The misfortune of the Irish is that they rose prematurely, when the European revolt of the proletariat had not yet matured. Capitalism is not so harmoniously built that the various springs of rebellion can immediately merge into one, of their own accord, without reverses and defeats.' Thus, D'Arcy and Arden imply, the story continues; Connolly's question

> The red flag of the peoples of the world
> Has no room in it for a single patch of green – ?

is also the question the play is asking; it is firmly directed at the Left, as the whole cycle is an attempt to share with the Left the terrible heritage of Britain's presence in Ireland. This, at present, is the question Arden feels he must go on asking. 'Ireland, for me now, is Pieter Bruegel's crowded market-place.'[17]

5
'Serjeant Musgrave's Dance'
and 'Ars Longa, Vita Brevis'

The eyes she borrowed from me
She returned to me once more
And I see a whole great waterscape
I never saw before.
(John Arden, *The Young Woman from Ireland*)

It is impossible in a volume this size to give a detailed analysis of the whole body of Arden's work. It is also impossible, with a living and working writer, to make a selection of the 'best' plays, or those most likely to endure. In this and the next chapter are analyses of four plays which I have chosen to represent his special quality on the

106

following grounds: they span the full extent of his career to date; they include two written alone, and two with D'Arcy; they are very different from one another, in style, length, and in terms of the production they have received. *Serjeant Musgrave's Dance*, for example, has been successfully interpreted in many ways, as I hope to show; *The Island of the Mighty* has been fraught with problems; *Ars Longa, Vita Brevis* has attracted amateurs and professionals, and I intend to deal with it in terms of my own experience in directing the play; *Pearl* shows Arden working successfully in a different medium, that of radio.

Serjeant Musgrave's Dance is staged more frequently than any other Arden play; he once remarked that it kept him in bread and butter. Five soldiers, led by Musgrave, come to a northern town gripped by snow and pit-strike, some time in the 1880s. They are ostensibly recruiting, although the miners are suspicious and the pit-owning mayor hopes to see the trouble-makers dealt with, or at least conned into taking the Queen's shilling. It is soon apparent to us that they are deserters with an anti-war lesson to teach. One of them, Sparky, is afraid, and tries to run; he is killed in a scuffle and the soldiers hide his body. Musgrave holds a meeting in the town, at which he hoists up on the market cross the skeleton of a local boy, Billy, killed in the colonial wars; then he turns a Gatling gun on the townspeople and tells them his 'logic': Billy was killed and five natives were executed in reprisal: twenty-five townspeople must now die, to bring the fight back to the place where it began. The other soldiers desert him; the barmaid Annie, Billy's girl, produces Sparky's jacket and the miners turn away too. Suddenly, like the US cavalry, the dragoons, desperately summoned by the Mayor to break the strike and contain possible riots, arrive and restore order at gunpoint. The townspeople join in a dance, ostensibly of celebration but surrounded by troops in red coats. Musgrave and the pacifist Private Attercliffe wait to be hanged, watched over by the owner of the inn, Mrs Hitchcock; and the curtain falls with Attercliffe singing a song about a rose and a green apple and asking Musgrave, 'They're going to hang us up a length higher nor most apple-trees grow, Serjeant. D'you reckon we can start an orchard?'

It is rare now to find a considered study of the play that does not start from the assumption that, despite flaws, it is one of the finest plays written in this country in the last three decades. However, critical interpretations vary widely. It has been seen as Arden's departure from naturalism, and as a partial return to it; as a picture of existence as 'senseless, absurd, useless'[1] and as showing Arden's 'adherence to a scale of values that are highly individual and at the same time interesting, wise and humane'.[2] This diversity suggests a very rich play indeed, and I hope to give some indication of its complex possibilities by examining several productions. First, however, I should like to look at the backbone of *Musgrave*: the images and patterns that remain constant throughout all the potential shifts and nuances of meaning and give the play its slashing authority.

Almost any critical analysis of *Serjeant Musgrave's Dance* quotes, with good reason, from *Telling a True Tale*: 'In the ballads the colours are primary. Black is for death, and for the coalmines. Red is for murder, and for the soldier's coat the collier puts on to escape from his black. Blue is for the sky and for the sea that parts true love. Green fields are speckled with bright flowers. The seasons are clearly defined. White winter, green spring, golden summer, red autumn.'[3] Anyone who reads or sees a production of the play carries away a strong impression of colours: red and black and white – and a small splash of green, the green apple of the final song. Arden assumes that his audience will have certain responses to these colours, responses rooted in ballad and legend; there can be few people who have never heard a song or a story which uses them in the way he describes. But he does not introduce them simply as trappings in order to hitch an easy emotional ride. Rather, he plays a whole series of variations upon them, he awakens new responses and makes us question old ones.

The soldiers' coats are red: the satirical Bargee, the play's bitter jester, quotes to them the old name for soldiers, derived not from their dress but from the stripes of the cat 'o'nine tails on their backs: 'Bloodred roses, that was it. What d'you think of that, eh? Whack, whack, whack.' In doing so he sums up the glamour and the pain of their profession. Red is also the colour of authority, that of the mayor's robes; it links him with the dragoons he uses to uphold it. Red is also the colour of blood, and in this play much blood is shed. Annie, caught up in the struggle which leads to the death of Sparky, finds his blood on her hands and licks it; when she cries out against Musgrave in the final act, it gives her authority: 'His blood's on my tongue, so hear what it says. A bayonet is a raven's beak. This tunic's a collier's jacket.' The blood is the same colour as the soldier's tunic – but it has turned it into the jacket of a collier, a man who lives in the town, not a stranger from the wars. The red and the black are united. Red is the colour of oppression, of the mayor and the dragoons, but it is also the colour of the oppressed, the blood-red roses and the starving miners. It is a compressed, complex image which carries a powerful emotional impact; it moves us but also forces us to think out its implications.

Similarly, black, the colour of death and of the Queen of Spades, the death card which keeps coming up in Sparky's card tricks, is also the colour of Black Jack Musgrave and his task: 'Our work isn't easy, no, and it's not soft: it's got a strong name – duty. And it's drawn out straight and black for us, a clear plan.' It is the colour of the colliers. Hence, the colour of death is also the colour of social change, through the pit-strike or through the message of Musgrave. The colour white, too, is used to make this paradoxical link: it is the colour of the snow that freezes up the town, of the skeleton of Billy, unchanging in death, but also the colour of the hottest fire of all, the white heat in which change can be forged: 'The winter's giving us one day, two days, three days even – that's clear safe for us to hold our time, take count of the corruption, then stand before this people with our white shining word, and let it dance! It's a hot coal, this town, despite that it's freezing – choose your moment and blow: and whoosh, she's flamed your roof off!' The complexity of the pattern that Arden weaves around the traditional colour-images adumbrates a society which is at once gripped by the most basic of needs – survival, love, passion, justice – the stuff of folk song – and so complicated that the expression of these needs cannot help but be agonizingly painful.

Other visual images work in the same way. The figure of the Soldier appears in countless ballads; he is usually a gay adventurer, attractive to women. In Sparky we have a similar figure, but he has another dimension. In this play the Soldier is the bearer of a terrible knowledge, he has seen the true face of war, and this darkens the picture of Sparky's attempts to captivate Annie. There is also the figure who appears in song and story, and on the Tarot cards – the Hanged Man. Hanging is the death of the proletarian hero in the old tales – Geordie, and Johnnie

110

Armstrong, and the young sailor in *Black-Eyed Susan*; aristocrats lose their heads. Linked to this image is another which haunted the art of Europe in the Middle Ages – the dancing skeleton, Death, who drew all humanity, king and beggar, into his dance. Here, the Soldier, Musgrave, is also the death-dancer as he stamps out his wild dance beneath the dangling Billy; the skeleton wears the jacket of the Soldier; both of them, in different ways, become the hanged hero. It is a complex pattern, which Andrew Kennedy describes thus: 'Even though this does evoke the remote-yet-familiar ballad world, it is felt as something "new". We have not heard just this rhythm, just these images before, and yet we hear echoes . . . in other words it is the kind of "imitation" that is recreation and not pastiche.'[4]

The visual images have an aural complement in the snatches of song and ballad Arden puts into the mouths of certain characters – not, it is important to note, the figures of authority, like the Mayor, the Parson and the Constable, who speak stolid prose peppered with clichés, but characters whose situation might figure in a ballad, characters for whom we might be expected to feel some sympathy or who give us an insight into the action. The function of the songs and ballads is to crystallize emotions which are too powerful for ordinary speech and also to extend their application. They express situations whose significance is eternal, not confined to the individual at present gripped by them; and they also comment upon these situations.

Take for instance the song sung by Attercliffe at the end of the play. It is the traditional story of the man who comes back to find his true love with another man, and is told

Your blood red rose is withered and gone
And fallen on the floor
And he who brought the apple down
Shall be my darling dear.

In this context the song takes on considerable resonance. It
is sung by a man who has lived out these symbols himself
and speaks from sharp experience. Attercliffe's wife left
him for a greengrocer. 'He was the best looker . . . or any
road that's what she said. I saw him four foot ten inch tall
and he looked like a rat grinning through a brush; but he
sold good green apples and he fed the people and he fed my
wife. I didn't do neither.' The experience underlying the
song gives it authority and this in turn pushes its
significance beyond that of an account of a lost love. It
becomes a song of stoical acceptance of a harsh fate and of
hope for the future, a hope that the mistakes made by the
'bloodred roses' in the town will still bear fruit, an
'orchard' of human dignity.

The play has strong links with the Morality tradition and
also with the medieval ritual dramas. Mary O'Connell has
found specific links with the Mummers Play of Plough
Monday, a play showing the death of winter and the birth
of spring, which even contains Musgrave's own line 'I'll go
north; I'm told it suits my character'.[5] Here the pattern of
death and resurrection is an ironic one; the dance at the
end of the play marks not the arrival of the new year but
the miners' return to work under the old conditions; the
death of Musgrave may not be in vain, but we do not know
for certain.

The pattern, however, gives the play a satisfying shape;
its powerful images sustain us through the slow and
suspenseful first two acts, in which we are not always
aware of what is going on; Arden subsequently felt that,

112

while the appearance of the skeleton is a splendid *coup de théâtre*, the general purpose of the soldiers could be clearer.[6] Even if we are not always clear as to the plot, however, we are aware of a very sharply defined community and the forces at work within it; these archetypal images of cold and dark and struggle versus love and energy are so firmly focused that we have a real sense of what it is like to live in such a time and place. The actual fleshing out of the strong bones of the play, however, leaves both actor and director with many interesting possibilities.

Productions of *Serjeant Musgrave's Dance* over the last twenty or so years have been very revealing in terms of prevalent attitudes to both theatre and society. The first production in 1959 at the Royal Court, and the most recent at the National Theatre in 1981, for instance, demonstrate a definite shift in the response of a British audience to stylization (not least in the fact that the former played to houses of about twenty per cent and the latter to capacity). Lindsay Anderson, in 1959, had sets by Jocelyn Herbert which kept faithfully to Arden's instructions. 'Scenery must be sparing – only those pieces of architecture, furniture and properties actually *used* in the action need be present: and they should be thoroughly realistic, so that the audience sees a selection from the details of everyday life rather than a generalised impression of the whole of it.'

Thus the first scene was played with only a drum and a few boxes; the second, in the pub, had a wall with a door and the fancy frosted glass windows typical of the period, as well as a bar and tables; the third, the churchyard where the soldiers encounter the miners, consisted of a few gravestones, a fence, and a twisted willow, the tree – as Annie later sings – of the deserted lover. The soldiers' sleeping quarters were shown in some detail; a fence with a lantern flanked three neat pallets, and a flight of steps led to the Serjeant's room with its big brass bed. The set for the recruiting meeting had, as Arden asked 'a sort of Victorian clock-tower-cum-lampost-cum market-cross' decked out with bunting and bright with Union Jacks. The final prison scene simply lowered half a dozen iron bars in front of the dancing townspeople, cutting off Musgrave and Attercliffe. Between the scenes, a gauze was lowered; lit from the front, it showed a mining town, huddled wintry houses dwarfed by the pit-hoist; lit from the back, it vanished before being raised. The effect was to act as a frequent reminder of the harsh economic realities of town life, giving weight to the viewpoint of the colliers; it also created a distancing effect, which Alan Brien described as 'half Ackerman print, half German silent film – remote, yet alive, in the centre of one of those crystal balls which foam into a snowstorm when you turn them upside down'.[7] It was a beautiful and evocative set which accorded well with the world created by the actors and the mixture of verse and prose, often backed by Dudley Moore's haunting music, eerie sustained high notes like a musical saw.

John Burgess's production at the Cottesloe Theatre in the National complex had an even simpler set, designed by Peter Hartwell. It was stripped to the barest of bones – drum and boxes, two graves, a bar; three mattresses and a bed on a plinth. The complicated market centre-piece was a simple cross. At the back was a white cyclorama which made no attempt to disguise itself as anything else; a plain white curtain whisked across between scenes which were changed very rapidly indeed, in contrast to the Court, whose lack of backstage facilities made this a slow business. The set, and the speed, suggested a confidence in the ability of the audience to do without all but the most basic visual clues, and also, perhaps, their television-trained unwillingness to endure long pauses. Similarly, the delivery of the verse speeches and ballads was easy and matter-of-fact, suggesting that the audience could be expected to feel at home in the convention. Audience address, too, was used without problems – for instance, in the graveyard scene Musgrave forces Sparky to state their purpose:

> MUSGRAVE: . . . We've come to this town to work that guilt back to where it began. (*He turns to Sparky*) Why to this town? Say it, say it!
>
> SPARKY: (*as with a conditioned reflex*) Billy. Billy's dead. He wor my mucker. Back end of the rear rank. He wor killed dead. He came from this town.
>
> MUSGRAVE: Go on.
>
> SPARKY: (*appealing*) Serjeant –
>
> MUSGRAVE: Use your clear brain, man, and tell me what you're doing here!

This is hard to play naturalistically; it can seem a very clumsy piece of exposition. In Burgess's production, the lines were delivered quite straightforwardly to the audience as a way of imparting information which they needed to know. Ewan Stewart as Sparky faced the front and spoke without any internal agonizing after psychological motivation. The whole production, in fact, trusted the audience to cope with a style that was not always naturalistic and, judging from the continuously full houses, this seems to have been justified.

Other differences were apparent, which spring from changes in the way we see society rather than theatrical conventions. The balance of the play is a complex one. There are so many groups juxtaposed – the soldiers, the

115

authority figures, the women, the colliers, and the always mocking Bargee. The broad lines are clear enough. The Mayor and his men can never be seen as representing anything but their own interests; Musgrave's threat to the lives of twenty-five innocent people can never be justified. But within these main moral lines many subtleties are possible.

Arden, writing about the play in 1960, was careful to stress the improbability of the plot; his sources were a single incident in Cyprus, when civilians were killed by troops running wild after the murder of a soldier's wife, and Hugo Fregonese's Western film, *The Raid.* Now the elaborate chess-game of bargaining and fighting over hostages is a frequent occurrence: after one incident people were interviewed and asked what they thought of the TV coverage; Musgrave's bit of Rough Theatre has become a world-wide participatory event. The play no longer seems improbable, and this naturally affects our response to it. Perhaps the most apt symbolic expression of this is the dance of John Thaw in 1981, contrasted with that of Ian Bannen in 1959.

Bannen was charged throughout with manic energy; he swung unnervingly between the matter-of-fact and roaring fury. Alan Brien described him as 'a soldier stuffed stiff with ramrods and gun-cotton, whose madness shines through only in restless eyes which swivel like greased ball-bearings'.[8] The word 'madness' appeared in more than one review, and the dance beneath the dangling skeleton reinforced the impression; the voice was at full volume, chanting the hypnotic rhymes, 'Up he goes and no-one knows/ How to bring him downwards', the feet stamped as if on some demonic parade, backed by drumbeats and a wailing note on the organ which suggested the inner working of a tortured mind. Then everything stopped at once, and Bannen grew quiet; the apparent drop into sanity made the exposition of his terrible 'logic' the more terrifying. His Musgrave was a figure of passionate authority, a mad avenging angel.

By contrast, Thaw's dance was less obviously striking. His movements were small and contorted; only after you had been watching for some time did it become clear that they were a dreadful parody of bayonet drill. The precision became chilling. This Musgrave did not shout; he was talking to himself, not his audience; his *coup de théâtre* was not an apocalyptic sermon but an agonized self-exposure, the more painful to watch because of the rigid reticence of the early acts.

Musgrave tells the townspeople that they have come from 'a little country without much importance except from the point of view that there's a Union Jack flies over it and the people of that country can write British subject after their names'. In 1959 this did not suggest a particular location; in 1981 it brought the shadow of Northern Ireland across the stage. Both productions made one of the soldiers Irish. In Anderson's version it was Sparky; the accent served to emphasize his loneliness, and the songs, sung to Irish airs with great artistry, made him a rather poetic figure. But Burgess's Irishman was Hurst, the soldier who says: 'It's time we did our own killing . . . we caught it overseas and now we've got to run round the English streets biting every leg to give it them.' The accent was Belfast rather than Dublin; it gave the group of soldiers a political complexity that is certainly latent in the play – Hurst turns the Gatling upon the authority figures, the Parson, the Mayor and the Constable, an idea not originated by Musgrave but one which has seldom been brought out so clearly.

The relative familiarity of the situation shown in the

117

play also gave the final scenes a slightly different emphasis. The moral centre of the play still lay with the women; this was stressed by the retention of a scene cut by Anderson, in which Annie climbs down a ladder from an upstairs window to cradle the skeleton of her man; here Elizabeth Estensen made a dramatic descent from the audience balcony, and its sheer perilousness gave great weight to her speeches. But it was also important that Musgrave, in fact, *killed* nobody; the only killing is done by the dragoon who shoots Hurst and, ironically, the pacifist Private Attercliffe. The scene in which Mrs Hitchcock visits him in jail took account of this. The main point which stood out from this scene in the earlier version was her account of where he had failed: '. . . last evening you told all about this anarchy and where it came from – like, scribble all over with life or love, and that makes anarchy. Right? . . . Look at it this road: here we are, and we'd got life and love. Then you came in and you did your scribbling where nobody asked you. Aye, its arsey-versey to what you said, but it's still an anarchy, isn't it?'

But this isn't all that she says, and in Burgess's production one of the memorable lines of the night was her prophecy: 'Those men are hungry, so they've got no time for you. One day they'll be full, though, and the Dragoons'll be gone, and then they'll remember.' It was a real promise, and in this context of certainty Attercliffe's song of the green apple was not just a general statement of hope but of faith in the spirit of their mission:

> For the apple holds a seed will grow
> In live and lengthy joy
> To raise a flourishing tree of fruit
> For ever and a day.

In the 1981 version it was Attercliffe rather than Sparky who was the accomplished singer. Peter Sproule's rendering of the song was a polished and conscious performance; Attercliffe was demanding our attention and making a clear assertion of faith. It will be interesting to hear the same song in twenty years' time – and to see the dance.

In contrast to the 1959 and 1981 productions are two which may be styled alternative versions, rather than interpretations of the original text. They show the hold that it has on the theatrical imagination and they also serve as valuable additions to the ever-increasing body of criticism. The first is Peter Brook's version at the Theatre Athénée in Paris, 1963. It concentrated heavily on ritual and violence. The skeleton in the market place became a magic centre for the energies of the whole work – what Brook describes in *The Empty Space* as a 'voodoo pole'[9]; the killing of Sparky was the sacrifice of one who had been marked as a victim from his first appearance; his death, rather than the hue-and-cry after the colliers who try to steal the Gatling, was the climax of the scene at the inn. It was an exciting production, but it blurred the precise sociological realism at the heart of the play. The set, for instance, consisted of abstract shapes in grey and green, so that Arden's idea of showing the concrete details of a way of life was lost; and the translation – inevitably – exacerbated this by its failure to find idiomatic equivalents for key phrases. For instance, after the murder of Sparky, the Bargee finds Musgrave alone, head in hands, and sings a mocking little song: 'Here we sit like birds in a wilderness'. It is a well known song, and rather resembles the First World War lament 'We're 'ere because we're 'ere because we're 'ere' in spirit. It acts as a puncturing voice in the atmosphere of despair surrounding Musgrave – and it also points up his integrity next to this man for whom nothing really matters. But the French version 'nous sommes deux oiseaux' totally lacked this dimension; any song would have done as well.

Brook also ended the play differently, bringing on the dancing colliers after the final scene. Thus it ended on a note of nihilism. Musgrave stood stage centre, his arms spread as if crucified; he seemed betrayed by the stupidity of the colliers rather than by his own inability to distinguish logic from justice. It may have been thrilling to watch, but it did great violence to the sharp concern with society that runs through the play.

John McGrath's *Serjeant Musgrave Dances On*, a new version written, partly at Arden's suggestion, in 1972 for the 7.84 company, was, in contrast to the Brook production, a response to a specific political situation; and it derived considerable impact from the 'classic' and A-level status of its original. In the winter of 1972 there was industrial trouble on the coalfields on a scale not seen since the General Strike. In Derry, thirteen people were shot down by the Paras. McGrath impacted both of these real events onto the story of Musgrave. The difference it made to the play is clear from the opening song:

There's a whole lot of trouble in this little town
The miners are up and they won't go back down.
We risk getting crushed every day of our lives
For food and for clothes for our kids and our wives –
And everybody reckons that's normal
The way it has to be – natural.

The song shows that the play will be approached from the miners' perspective. It also has a function very different from Arden's songs and the oblique illumination they provide: there is, here, no attempt to be objective; it hits hard at the Coal Board and demands our support and involvement – the last two lines form a sardonic chorus for us to join in. The mocking Bargee was also omitted, and the miners given more political understanding of the situation. While, in 1959, one of the striking moments was the conclusion to Musgrave's prayer that God will 'keep my mind clear so I can weigh Judgement against the Mercy and Judgement against the Blood' and the Bargee's mocking 'Amen' in parody, the 'Amen' in McGrath's version was given to a miner quietly swinging his pick in the shadows. Allusions throughout to the strike and the Industrial Relations Act made it clear that support was sought for a particular cause.

Musgrave was less helpful to the miners than his original. The scene in which he hides the would-be thieves of the Gatling from the Law was omitted. He had one main message – to relate, in detail, the shooting down of the Derry Thirteen. The effect was electrifying. It did, however, create some problems. For instance, it was hard to respond to the skeleton of the fictional Billy in the face of those thirteen terrible realities. The rejection of Musgrave by the miners – despite their eminently sane criticism of his 'individualistic, uncoordinated tactics', and their lucid exposition of their own fight – tended to leave the problem created by those thirteen names in mid-air. As they went out to deal with 'the pit-men, the dockers, the builders, the shipyard men – that's to do with real life', it seemed that Ireland was being left firmly in the theatre and that the Left were being encouraged to ignore it, at least for the present. Nevertheless, the play had a powerful impact and it affirmed, yet again, the strength of the original *Serjeant Musgrave's Dance*.

On the surface *Ars Longa, Vita Brevis* looks like a very

simple play. It was written by Arden and D'Arcy for two specific groups – some local children at Kirbymoorside, and Peter Brook's group formed to explore the ideas of Artaud in his Theatre of Cruelty season at the London Academy of Music and Dramatic Art (LAMDA) in 1963– 64. The story grew out of a newspaper cutting about the accidental shooting of a teacher during some Territorial Army manoeuvres in a wood, and a box of old clothes found by the children. It has seven short scenes. In the first, the Headmaster of St Uncumbers School makes a speech introducing the new art master, Mr Miltiades. In the second, he interviews him and is gratified to find that he is a vehement opponent of free expression. In the third, Mr Miltiades tries to teach his class to draw; the lesson develops into drill and finally into a battle, interrupted by the headmaster who is not impressed. In the fourth, Miltiades complains to his wife and ends up running off with the Territorial Army. In the fifth, the soldiers disguise themselves as trees. In the sixth, the headmaster goes shooting with the school governors and shoots Miltiades, pretending to think that he is a deer. Miltiades laments his fate in verse like a Jacobean tragic hero and dies. In the seventh, his widow is consoled with money which enables her to enjoy herself with young men and fast cars; she speaks a lament as 'in the middle of her enjoyment' she encounters his coffin on its way to the churchyard.

Artaud was primarily concerned with the non-verbal, emotional values of theatre; despite the fact that Arden and D'Arcy were happy for the actors to improvise to a great extent within the framework of the plot, it examines the relationship between war, art and education in ways that provoke thought and laughter rather than the irrational and subconscious reactions that Artaud's theatre looks for. It is, however, an admirable play to work on within a context of learning such as the Brook experimental season, because it provides the actor with many interesting challenges. D'Arcy once said that she had learned a lot about theatre from her children – that, in fact, you can see that natural actor in all of us when you watch a small child enter a room. *Ars Longa, Vita Brevis* is designed to liberate in the actor the energy and inventiveness of children's play. It forces attention away from psychological issues and forces you to concentrate on the action, and how to perform it: and this in turn forces you to look at the patterns of energy informing the play, which prove to be very complex indeed.

I worked on this play with students beginning a university course in drama. Their experience varied very widely – some had acted for years, others had never been on a stage; most of them, however, tended to use exclusively the vocabulary of theatrical naturalism, and part of the purpose of the play was to confront them with a very different convention.

We began – as most groups who work on the play – by playing games, partly because they broke the ice and also because they fitted the theme of the play. We found that the games fell into three groups. Rough and tumble, like tag and British Bulldog, loosened people up and liberated a great deal of energy. These helped them to move freely and to shout without strain, and they reflected the aggression of the battle scenes. Ritualistic games, like Oranges and Lemons and the Farmer in his Den, were basically about precision and discipline, but, when we came to look at them clearly, all contained elements of violence. In other games the object is to outwit the figure in authority, such as Grandmother's Footsteps, and What's the Time, Mr Wolf? The most interesting game in this category was Simon Says, in which one person dictates to the rest exactly what they must do; as long as the instructions are prefaced by the words 'Simon Says' the participants have to obey absolutely; if they are not, the participants have to remain still. The paradox of the game is that you can only win by doing exactly what you are told.

We went on to explore the relationship between teacher and class; the students playing 'teacher' soon discovered that, given that status, it was not difficult to impose your will on an individual with the status of 'pupil', but that you became shockingly vulnerable before a group of 'children' with a strong group identity. But in most classrooms the teaching cannot take place at all unless the children *do* have a strong group identity; consequently the 'teachers' constantly found themselves imposing discipline on individuals by forcing them to conform to a group spirit, which once created had the power to destroy them. One game that we used in the final production was a sort of guerrilla version of Simon Says: as Miltiades tried to conduct his drawing lesson, the children disrupted things; first a giggle began to go round the class, and he ordered them to stop, so they did; then somebody began to rock in his chair, then another, then another, until he told them to stop, so they did; then they began passing rude pictures, until he told them to stop . . . the point was that they would always obey him, but always invent something fresh, and that they would all collaborate on every new bit of disobedience without the need to speak to one another at all. While we had started with the assumption that Mr Miltiades stood for repression and the children for anarchy, in practice the roles were reversed. (Albert Hunt had the same experience in producing the play.) The stricter the discipline from without, the more organized and dangerous the children became, and the more vulnerable the master. When he started the drill, he was able to control them only while they did it badly; once they had learned it, they became a threat; they ended up goose-stepping towards him in an elaborate formation he had never ordered, stamping out and drumming a fierce rhythm and stopping only inches from him while he tried to pretend they were obeying his orders. As they moved into the battle scene, he became more and more excited, finally screaming 'Kill! Kill!' as the headmaster entered to find a disciplined body of children in charge of a teacher apparently gone berserk.

As Arden and D'Arcy suggest, the children all wore masks, very simple shapes of yellow cardboard; many of them, especially the less experienced actors, found them liberating. The effect was eerie; no matter how ferocious the action, the faces remained austere, impassive. This effect reinforced the impression of power among this apparently oppressed group; it also pointed up the central paradox – the actors playing Miltiades and the headmaster chose not to wear masks, and this choice stressed the fact that the chief disciplinarians of the play were also its rabid individualists. The girl playing the headmaster concluded her opening speech by calling for three cheers – a group effort – but as she began 'hip hip hip za huzza . . .' she got carried away and went off into a sort of verbal jazz which the masked children watched, silent. In the interview the two teachers became lyrical about what is ultimately an act of deprivation:

ART MASTER: Firm groundwork in drawing. Set a few pots, oranges, a still life, an old mangle, a newspaper, a bowler hat, a can or bucket, a tin of peaches, on the table. Make them draw it. Then after that progress to plaster casts. Heads of Caesar, Alexander, Young Augustus, Venus de Milo.

John Arden

HEADMASTER: Head only.

ART MASTER: Head. No arms. Arms quite available anyway from other sources. There's an Athene, in a tunic, helmet, shield, very suitable. Make them draw it.

HEADMASTER: In pencil.

Miltiades is like a parody of Musgrave in his earnest desire for a duty drawn out clear and black; but he lacks Musgrave's fidelity to an idea, however misguided, underlying that discipline. Ravished by the idea of joining the Territorials, he puzzles the recruiting officer by his demands for the 'glowing brutalities' of the army. The officer, failing to sell him the idea of technological warfare and family allowances for the Forces, concludes glumly 'all you're fit for is soldiering'. It is a multi-faceted look at the idea of war; war is a disciplined activity, but it cannot take place without an aggression that is the apparent reverse of discipline. The Army may prefer to stress the many benefits of being a soldier, but they are still recruiting men who may get killed as a result of enlisting. The play articulates a similar paradox about art. Miltiades's approach to art destroys its very essence, but he points out to his wife an undeniable fact about the need for disciplined artists – 'Look at Leonardo da Vinci – he painted the Last Supper and it fell off the wall. Why? because he had forgotten that he once had been a military engineer.' On the other hand, art itself creates anarchy in real life; Miltiades is shot while acting the part of a tree, by a headmaster acting the part of a deer hunter – but the bullet is real. We played the scene in a green spotlight and a rather balletic style, but with realistic blood to counterpoint the theatricality of the dying speech, which itself makes a point about life and art – that the

126

Territorials, the mock-soldiers, have engineered a real killing:

> Technology is confounded and art takes its place
> For here I have received a real bullet in my face.
> Hardihood and discipline
> Straight lines and repression
> Have today found their old true expression;
> I die for my duty and I die with a smile
> The Territorial Army has proved itself real.

Like *Serjeant Musgrave's Dance*, the play also looks at another relationship – that between discipline and love. Mrs Miltiades encourages her husband to discuss his discipline in the classroom while trying anarchically to seduce him: 'You must preserve discipline. Did you not preserve it, my love, my chick, my chuck, my piggeseye, my little apple dumpling, my sweet cake, my cherry tart, my pretty little Christmas tree?' She can enjoy herself after his death, but her farewell speech, while rejecting all he stood for, manages to invest his memory with a sort of posthumous sensuality by its lyrical grace:

> I shed a tear upon his bier
> Because to me he was ever dear.
> But I could not follow him in all his wishes
> I prefer the quick easy swimming of the fishes
> Which sport and play
> In green water all day
> And have not a straight line in the whole of their bodies.

Ars Longa, Vita Brevis works because its spirit is childlike. It is not about games, although games always seem to help actors in working on it; rather, it is about play. Play is a serious activity: children pretend to be other people, other things, but they do so by telling the truth as they see it. Here the subjects are serious – in fact, they are the stuff of life and death; and the truths which Arden and D'Arcy force out of their hiding places in this freewheeling and energetic comedy are complex indeed.

6
'The Island of the Mighty' and 'Pearl'

'In the Welsh Codes of Court Procedure the Bard of the Household is instructed to sing to the Queen when she goes to her chamber to rest. He is instructed to sing first to her a song in honour of God. He must then sing the song of the Battle of Camlann – the son of treachery and of the undoing of all things.'[1]

On the whole, works about King Arthur and his death in Camlann have taken two forms in recent years: the archeological, attempting to find the 'reality' behind the 'myth', and the romantic, firmly centring on the Arthur–Lancelot–Guinevere triangle. As David Jones shows, however, the legend has tended in the past to have a political function; this was exploited not only by the Welsh Bards, but by Malory, who tried to demonstrate through it

129

the feudal virtues he saw the barons of his time trying to erode, and by the peasants who clung to the hope of Arthur's eventual return to save them from oppression – a rumour neatly squashed by the Glastonbury monks who conveniently discovered his grave and made their fortunes in the process. Arden and D'Arcy, looking at the story in 1972 from a Marxist perspective, were thus part of a long-established tradition; if this had been more clearly understood at the time, much of the controversy over the play need never have happened.

The year of the political troubles described in relation to *Serjeant Musgrave Dances On* and *The Ballygombeen Bequest*, 1972, was a watershed year for Arden. He was entering his forties, for many writers a period of consolidation rather than innovation; for him, it marked the establishment of a new phase in his work, his increasing concentration upon the matter of of Ireland and his use of theatres outside the conventional circuit. In the trilogy, *The Island of the Mighty*, it also saw the culmination of the work of many years. He had been working on an Arthur play since his schooldays; one version was rejected by the Royal Court in 1956 (the reader's report read 'boring historical play written in phoney verse') and later he worked on a television trilogy, eventually shelved, which provided the characters and structure for the final version of 1972.

A note in the programme for the Royal Shakespeare Company production states the intentions behind that version:

National myths of this sort present a picture of a way of life remarkably similar to that which exists today in the "Third World" – by which I mean those parts of the globe that have been occupied and exploited by one or other of the great modern empires. Just as the energy of Britain in the sixth century was concentrated among the wild tribesmen of the hills and the crude English just stepped from their black ships, so the third world contains – to our alarm and perhaps our ultimate salvation – the strongest urge for social change and the keenest courage in bringing it about . . . we have attempted no more than to indicate – from a rocking and sinking post-imperialist standpoint (for what else is the stage of a subsidised London theatre in 1972?) – something of how the early history of Britain foreshadows twentieth century turbulence. 'King Arthur is nat dede' – but he seems to have changed sides. The true voice of liberty is more likely to be heard today from the kind of men and women who have little part to play in the traditional tales: I mean the ones who did the work, who fed and housed the noble warriors, and who equipped them for their fight.

The plays spend, as we shall see, a lot of time with 'the ones who did the work', and this lies at the root of the Aldwych dispute. The director, David Jones, related in an interview his initial misgivings about the length of the piece, and how the final decision hinged on 'whether John Arden and Margaretta D'Arcy felt that it was feasible to make a single evening's entertainment out of the three parts . . . we found that the third part was in many ways a coda to the main action and could possible be dispensed with . . . the most severe cuts have been in the third part'.[2] The cuts, from several points of view, were a drastic mistake. First, the plays are a *trilogy*; this is a form used since the Ancient Greeks and still popular on television; it gives the writer a chance to explore a theme in depth, from more than one point of view, while retaining a tight and disciplined structure. The audience can be confronted with hard analysis or eventful action without becoming exhausted, because they are given, three times, a definitive resting-point and a chance to reassess what they have seen. The Royal Shakespeare Company production, however, became a long play with pauses; the structure became confused and of the many reviews which commented on the fact, most of them stressed that the problem arose in the second half of the evening, where the severest cuts had been made. The *Guardian*, for instance, found the four-hour experience 'unwieldy, inchoate and exasperating'[3] and *Tribune* found it 'full of digressions' although 'splendidly rich'[4] – problems which might have disappeared if the three plays had been seen in full over more than one day.

The second problem created by the cuts was one of focus. The truncated shape made the play an 'Arthuriad' rather than the study of a whole society that Arden and D'Arcy had written. The trilogy has a clear structure: the first part concentrates on two young men, Balin and Balan, and their experience of that society; the second, upon Arthur's marriage and the Battle of Camlann in which he and his incestuous son Medraut kill each other (this is the only part of the trilogy to which the authors attach the label 'concerning Arthur'); the third part is about Merlin. The balance thus created makes 'the people who did the work', encountered by the young men and Merlin, the real centre of the play; the truncated version made Arthur the 'hero' at their expense; this led to the 'imperialistic' cast of the play complained of by Arden and D'Arcy.

These problems were exacerbated by the style of the performance. Albert Hunt, who attended rehearsals, found a continual preoccupation with the Stanislavskian approach.[5] Arthur became a totally sympathetic character with whom the audience could identify, not a figure who has to be judged, sometimes harshly, by the audience. The action, instead of proceeding rapidly as the authors wanted, slowed down as characters groped for motivation. Details crept in that worried Arden – for instance, a scene in which the bandit Garlon beats up his woman took on totally different connotations as he whipped her with his belt; a statement about economic relationships had become a sexual scene – 'all the difference in the world'.[6]

An analysis of the play, therefore, really has to depend upon the printed text rather than the illumination provided by a performance true to the authors' intention. However, Arden and D'Arcy have been at some pains to describe the style they wanted, and the published edition is full of useful advice to future directors.

The Indian experience pervades the trilogy; it not only reflects the newly awakened political concern Arden found there, but the profound influence of a new culture upon Arden and D'Arcy alike. In Bengal, they found plays which operated on a time-scale quite different from that of Western theatres. They ran for anything up to a week, using complex but familiar mythologies; Arden liked to think he had experienced something rather akin to the feeling of a York craftsman watching a medieval guild play. They were very stylized, making extensive use of masks which are in themselves very beautiful and elaborately made. It is a special skill, to which whole villages devote themselves. There were long dances, full of energy and accompanied by much noise. Arden recalls dozing off during an all-night performance and occasionally waking to hear 'the same continuous stamping up and down of proud spangled giants'.[7] The richness and energy of the plays and their uninhibited delight in spectacle was a strong influence on *The Island of the Mighty*. It is also perhaps clear from the description that these are plays which are not meant to be 'done properly'; they are performed for pleasure and worship, not as professional entertainment. Indeed Arden has written with some bitterness of the poverty of the performers and their frequent exploitation by the tourist trade. It was perhaps inevitable that techniques learned in the Third World would find themselves in a peculiar relationship with the Royal Shakespeare Company of the early 70s, heavily subsidized and rich in technological wizardry, in danger of becoming, in Colin Chambers's trenchant phrase, 'the ICI of the theatre'.[8] It is tempting to wonder what might have happened if the plays had been staged in the later 70's when the small shoestring theatres of the Royal Shakespeare Company, the Other Place and the Warehouse, began to develop.

They might have captured, in their intimate spaces, some of the pace that the authors wanted. They urge a speed of twenty lines a minute. It is worth pointing out that there are many outdoor scenes, set in weather that is both wild and cold. This also suggests very brisk playing indeed, much as the first scene of *Hamlet* needs to reflect, by its speed, the fact that 'the air bites shrewdly'. They also wanted the actors to be, quite clearly, actors, and to play upon a platform, a stage upon a stage, while other actors remained present and not necessarily 'in character'. They demand skills in dancing, tumbling and swordfighting. Everything on stage should have a purpose. Clothes show the social position of the wearer and should also, to reflect the period, be brightly coloured, which makes the play visually vibrant. Properties, as always in Arden's work, should be restricted to those actually needed – Arthur's battle-standard, a multi-layered symbol, is a good example. There is a great deal of music, not only songs, but as background to the action. There are elaborate masks in the Indian style. In fact, the play is full of colour, energy and spectacle; it is highly stylized while conveying in sharp detail a whole society and a critique of it. It is a bold concept and one which has not yet received full credit for that boldness; a full realization of the play in the style Arden and D'Arcy hoped for might become a piece of 'rough theatre' of a very exciting kind.

The Island of the Mighty shows an empire menaced from without and crumbling from within. Throughout the play there is the constant threat of an English invasion; we hear about the brutality of these fighters from over the water, but we never see them. Instead, we see the internal struggles of the land. Arthur exemplifies all the rectilinear Roman virtues; he has read Tacitus and Livy and fights by the book. He says his prayers; he is also autocratic, intolerant, and haunted by his own pagan past. Set against the Romanized world of Arthur is a tribal society, savage and primitive. In its purest form it is symbolized by the Picts, a group Arthur would dearly love to forget, but through neighbouring princes and their squabbles he is forced to negotiate – and eventually fight – with them. They have a secret, savage, matriarchal underlife, often repugnant in its violence, but also full of vitality and the potential for change. The Pictish values are also the old .values of Arthur's world, and they are present, to some extent, in his followers and his queen, and are deeply buried in his own soul. As these two forces struggle for possession, two groups of people have to deal with the consequences – the peasants, who have to survive, and the poets, who have to make political sense of it all.

The first part of the trilogy, *Two Wild Young Noblemen*, presents us with two lads who have to reassess their position in society, thus providing the audience with a great deal of information. They have lost everything in an English raid, and at the beginning of the play are fighting each other in impotent fury. This makes them a fitting symbol of the land as a whole; they have abundant energy, but no knowledge as to the best way to direct it. As they quarrel and split, they experience all the possible sources of power in the country. We are invited to judge these sources for ourselves.

Balin chooses to take Arthur for his leader. His ancestors fought the Romans, and he expects to find in him a legendary and awesome dragon-slayer (perhaps, at this point, the audience does so too). What he finds is a lame old man, trying to draw strength from Roman discipline to keep him going. Balin witnesses one of the most important confrontations of the trilogy, between Arthur and the Ambassador of the Picts. Arthur does not want to handle this, but is forced into it by his cousin Strathclyde, who sees his permanent feud with the Picts as more important than the imminent invasion. We see two cultures meet head-on. Arthur hides behind a golden Apollo mask, classically beautiful; his language is careful, measured, the tool of a skilled negotiator. The Pict expresses herself through dance and mime, through cryptic utterances by her Poet, through her tattooed skin and the fur of the cat that she wears as her tribal emblem. The contrast is striking, and the tension between the central figures almost unbearable. Balin snaps this tension; he kills the Ambassador, and precipitates a war. In doing so, and in siding with Arthur, he has dangerously misdirected his energy. Through these negotiations we learn that the Picts are starving. They accuse the petty Strathclyde of genocide. Starving as they are, however, they have far greater vitality than Arthur, tottering on his stick; and their painful experience is like Balin's own – they are his natural allies.

Balan experiences another side of Pictish society; he falls into their hands and in an old and bloody ritual becomes their king for a year. Readers of *The Golden Bough*, and of the book which has profoundly influenced Arden in this play, *The White Goddess*, will recognize the figure of the Year King, whose function is to die to ensure that the crops will continue to grow. But in this play the idea is developed, not simply inserted as a bit of picturesque primitivism. Certainly the dark eroticism of the scene gets its full weight; the fight between the old king and the new is a splendidly costumed dance of death, and the verse in which the Pictish princess celebrates Balan has a sinewy beauty:

> Broad chest, short body
> No beard, hair like fire –
> Eyes as pale as the briar rose flower.

But this is a changing society; the Pictish war leader tries to persuade the queen that good men are needed for the war, that the ritual is pointless. When Balin too finds his way to the Picts, and fights his brother to their mutual death, the Poet articulates this change: 'We make our King lame so that he cannot escape. And then after all his pleasuring the next King finds it easy to kill him. Until now the custom was good. But certain of our people came to believe it should be put an end to, and I think that that is what the Goddess has now done.'

The Picts, then, are capable of development; but at present they have no real political direction. Balin also encounters another possible leader of the country, with equal vitality – the Bandit Garlon and the woman he has taken from the poet Taliesin. Garlon (who in the *Morte D'Arthur* is a knight), knows what he wants: 'I have suffered far too much from these Kings and these Princes. Every one of them is my enemy.' He wants only an end to the crippling taxes and the poverty inflicted by greedy noblemen. He has taught the Bondwoman his values. She tells Balin 'If you must live a life of fighting, why not fight in defence of me? There are so many like myself – everything that is ever done in the name of God or good order becomes done against us.'

But Balin kills Garlon, and the Bondwoman too dies in a scuffle. The play ends with many lessons learned, but learned, it seems, too late. Balin rejects the status of 'nobleman' which mattered so much to him at the start of the play, and dies encouraging the Picts to fight the Romanized leaders:

> . . . they are such old men
> Strapped up with hooks of iron.
> It should not be at all impossible
> For you to knock them out of their saddles.

But the Princess feels that the changes have come at the wrong time for war:

> How can we think we can win it
> When we don't know who we are?

Arthur in his Roman armour speaks the last speech of Part One; in his habitual colourless prose he harangues the audience about the need to preserve Roman values. At the beginning of the play, this would have seemed a speech fit for a tragic hero. As it is, we see the old order as repressive and enervated; we see a potential new order, but we are also aware how limited it is. The choice is not easy, but it is clearly death to cling to the past.

Part Two, *Oh, The Cruel Winter*, shows pagan values beneath the surface of Arthur's world. In Medraut, we have a character who has been educated in Roman values but who wishes to explore his native culture, just as a Sandhurst-trained young leader from the Third World might react against an exclusively British culture in his own country. He commands a horde of wild tribesmen called the 'Hounds of Bran' after the god-hero whose buried head is said to protect the island. He is thus, apparently, the antithesis of Arthur, who tells Merlin that he dug up the skull of Bran and carries it on his battle-standard in defiance of superstition.

Arthur depends on Medraut's vitality and youth; he cannot, however, bear to relinquish command to him. When an alliance is suggested between Medraut and the wayward sister of Prince Gododdin, Gwenhwyvar, Arthur's vanity leads him to marry her himself. On their wedding night, we see his dry Roman values confronted by her dark sexuality; they dance, a strange masked wild dance; and in the morning she puts the conflict into words:

Observe this disappointed man
Believes himself to be the fresh cold rain
And sunshine that will make the grass grow green.
He stretches out his corded arms and cries:
'Young woman, young woman strip off your clothes
Upon my scaly breast lay down your head.
I am the only champion of God.
Permit yourself to be split in two –'
The sword of Magnus Maximus goes through and through
The blood flows down between the knocking knees
And where it soaks into the ground so dry

The golden corn shall rise up thick and high
The fruits and flowers miraculously arise
All creatures that God made
Into this new-made garden come and feed . . .
So too in the trap-hole of the night you cried
You also cried. I was awake, I heard –
The dragon's mouth fell open and there fell out certain
words –
Do you remember what they were?

As the rich imagery suggests, the challenge is on a spiritual
as well as a sexual level. Gwenhwyvar learns from Arthur's
ancient sister Morgan what she has instinctively felt – that
she is a daughter of Branwen, a claimant to the ancient
matriarchal throne. She has to choose a consort, and she
takes not Arthur but Medraut, marking his forehead with
her nail in the sign of the horned moon. Medraut is now
ready to challenge the might of Arthur. As Arthur's power
crumbles, he faces at last his own pagan roots: he himself
was chosen by a daughter of Branwen; he was lamed not in
battle but in ritual, and he carries on his forehead the
mark of the horned moon; he has slept with his sister and is
Medraut's true father, as well as the lame and dying king
of the island, the spiritual equal of Balin and Balan. At the
Battle of Camlann, father and son kill each other and the
English slaughter indiscriminately; all is chaos.

The play looks at the breakdown and decay of the
energy of Arthur's world, at the sources of power failing
and drying up. Medraut, intelligent and young, gets
bogged down in a dream of pagan power and a return to
old ways; the strength of Gwenhwyvar goes to waste. Early
in the play she talks with her lover Aneurin and her maid
Gwenddyd about a mythical past:

GWENDDYD: She told me that this land was once inhabited by huge ladies of great beauty.

GWENHWYVAR: Huge?

ANEURIN: When they walked through the forest, with the scrape of their rolling hips the tree-tops were broken off. The print of their feet created mountain tarns full of frogs and little fishes, the red eagles flew in and out of the tangles of their long hair, and when they shed tears it came down like storms of rain.

But she is incapable of translating the matriarchal vision into terms which mean anything in the society she lives in; she can *do* nothing but choose her consort, the essentially reactionary Medraut. She may challenge Arthur, but her energy is all destructive. Roman and pagan values have finally collaborated in destroying an entire society.

Part Three, *A Handful of Watercress*, draws together the threads of a theme which runs through the whole trilogy, one which Arden felt to be of crucial importance and which he explored in most of his early versions of the Arthur story: that of the relationship of the poet to society. The work contains three poets: Taliesin, official bard to the unimaginative warmongering Prince of Strathclyde, who composes within a well defined tradition and is conservative in outlook; Aneurin, a subversive and sexy wanderer; and the ambiguous figure of Merlin.

Merlin, like Lindsay in *Armstrong's Last Goodnight*, is a wily diplomat, a wheeler and dealer. He sees his art as an important and lofty function:

> By reason of the working
> Of the words within his brain
> He moves among the minds of men
> Like sunlight or like moonlight

Like high wind or dark rain –
Changing the visible face of nature,
He disturbs the proud heart
Of each perceptive human creature,
And therefore by all, save unregulated devils,
He is preserved from mortal evils.
And his wisdom and his charity
Are accorded great authority.

This is in sharp contrast to his behaviour. He exists largely to prop up the *status quo*, to praise Arthur's generalship even while he sees its inadequacy; he belongs nowhere. When Arden began to create his Merlin in the mid-60s he saw him as 'the liberal intellectual who no longer knows what is liberality and what is tyranny, who is unable to draw a distinction between poetic ambiguity and political dishonesty' – the kind of person he felt to be much in evidence at a time when experimental theatre tended to be a multi-media sensual experience rather than a tool of political analysis, a distraction from the less acceptable aspects of the major Western power blocs. Merlin justifies himself with the classic concentration camp excuse 'I did obey, it was my trade'. He does not fit into the traditional mould of Taliesin, who is secure in his patriotic and Christian convictions, because he is too sophisticated; but he is also too involved with Arthur's world to share the Blakean vision of Aneurin's song of John the Baptist:

John Baptist out of the desert walked
And all he wore was a cloth of hair
And all he could cry was 'Beware beware –
The naked man has come to steal your coat!'

He met with Jesus by the river
And Jesus was dressed in cloth-of-gold
John Baptist tore it off and left him shivering cold –
John Baptist's head was served on a dish for the
    King's dinner.

Who fetched the King's soldiers to run him in?
Lord Jesus who was both Priest and King,
Who forgave the rich men all their sins
So long as they said that they loved him
And would whip their people till they loved him too –
Lord Jesus, a great revenge is coming upon you!

At Camlann, Merlin stabs Taliesin, who is trying to stop
the battle; Merlin believes that it should happen, that
Arthur should win – but he does nothing positive to help
him to do so. Taliesin curses him, and for the rest of the
play Merlin's fate is that of Crazy Sweeney, whose story is
told in *The White Goddess*. Robert Graves cites the triad
that sums up his tragedy:

> It is death to mock a poet
> It is death to love a poet
> It is death to be a poet.[9]

Merlin, like Sweeney, goes mad and thinks he has sprouted
feathers; he leaps high calling himself a bird. Like
Sweeney, he is befriended by a peasant woman, a
cowman's wife who gives him milk; the cowman thinks the
worst, and kills him – but Sweeney regains his sanity
before he dies. Merlin, coming out on the other side of
madness, regains his true poetic voice. Much of the third
play is taken up with the dully dutiful Bedwyr's efforts to
maintain the old Arthurian order, and his attempts to get

hold of Merlin and make him official bard. It is a bitterly comic episode; the chases are full of slapstick humour, but they take place across a waste land, vividly evoked, where the farms are dying because the water is poisoned with corpses. Both men eventually realize that the Roman general and the poet-negotiator have no place in the new world. Bedwyr throws away Arthur's sword and becomes a sort of holy man; Merlin is brought back to himself by his old love, Morgan. She represents the female principle his tight Roman Christianity had denied. Whole again, he makes a simple verse about the smile of the cowman's wife, and dies happy in the friendship that his verse has created.

Aneurin, the last surviving poet, grasps the significance of Merlin's conversion. He has made songs to teach the people – with some success, for Garlon sings the song of the Baptist and admires it – but he has seen his vocation as that of a lonely, rather superior figure. Now he sees that the relationship between poet and people is closer to that between Merlin and the cowman's wife than to the master-and-pupil idea promulgated by the college of bards. 'The poet without the people is nothing. The people without the poet will still be the people. . . . All that we can do is to make loud and to make clear their own proper voice. They have so much to say.' At the close of the play he sings a song about and for the people, resembling the song about the 'fat men of the fat-half world' of *The Ballygombeen Bequest.* It is a promise that things will be different, that the crushed and oppressed will eventually take the world for their own.

The Island of the Mighty was one of the most ambitious theatre projects of the last fifty years, both in terms of its scale and of the magnitude of the themes which it handles. It makes a serious attempt to explore British and Irish myths, and to ground these myths in a real society. We are able to acknowledge them as spiritual truths, and at the same time to see their limitations. The story of the Waste Land and the Lame King, for instance, are powerful and evocative stories with considerable resonance for British and Irish readers – but here they are set in a political context. The Waste Land, in this play, is not a magical place or a spiritual state, but a real land which the peasants have to work; it has been created by the king himself, and the way to heal it is not by magic but by the hard reality of social change. Similarly the Bard, the mystic figure so profoundly discussed in *The White Goddess*, here has his work redefined; instead of a privileged and apolitical servant of the Muse, he is the servant of the people who must live through the events he sings about, challenge them and change them. He must deal in analysis as well as vision.

Merlin becomes a bird, and the birds which appear most often in the trilogy are crows or ravens. The crow was the bird of Bran, a symbol of healing. In the twentieth century, it recalls two birds of a rather different feather – Ted Hughes's *Crow*, the cynical observer of a schizophrenic humanity, whose chief triumph is to survive, and the Green Crow, as Sean O'Casey liked to call himself, the political playwright who asserted fertility and joy as well as Marxism. It is a fitting symbol for a play with such an unprecedented mythological and political scope.

Pearl is one of Arden's finest plays to date; and a very paradoxical play it is. It was performed in 1978, when Arden's critical reputation was at a low ebb after *The Non-Stop Connolly Show* and his activities with the Galway Theatre Workshop, and was generally acknowledged as a masterpiece. It was performed in a medium for which it was not originally conceived, that of radio; and yet it not only received a Giles Cooper award for one of the best radio works of the year but, I believe, made a significant contribution to that medium. It was performed under the aegis of the BBC, the body which felt that a Connolly play would 'inflame passions', although much of it is taken up with a passionate and profound analysis of Anglo–Irish politics at a crucial point in history.

In some ways, radio as a playwright's medium resembles the stage of Shakespeare and Jonson. It invites the listener to use his or her imagination; we can be transported from Rome to Egypt, heaven to hell, in the space of a few lines; the words are the only scenery needed. One would expect a writer as steeped in the Jacobeans as Arden to use radio with great success. There is, however, another aspect of radio which makes his choice of it more unlikely.

When the Jacobean actor stood on the stage and said he was in Rome, the audience all agreed, tacitly, that they would go on acknowledging the stage as Rome as long as he stood there. He wore a costume which gave them a visual reminder, he walked with the gait of a Roman soldier, and there may well have been large and solid properties to reinforce the convention. If a radio actor says the word 'Rome' we have, momentarily, a mental image, but then the word has gone; nothing remains; the author will have to keep reminding us where the action is set. Or perhaps not. We have made our decision to imagine 'Rome' on evidence that is literally hearsay, a kind of evidence to which the law quite rightly attaches little value. It is open to the radio author to change the scene at will, to present us with a totally different reality. Perhaps 'Rome' exists only in the mind of the character who was speaking; perhaps a second character will later inform us that the scene is *really* being performed in a mental hospital. If so, whom do we believe? In both cases, our only evidence is those words that trembled on the air and vanished.

Consequently it is not surprising that the most successful radio playwrights of the last thirty or so years have been those who presented a universe which has no consistent reality, where life is unpredictable and lacking in coherence; Beckett, for instance, excels as a writer for radio. The work of the Absurdists found a natural home there. Writers like Giles Cooper and Barry Bermange exploited with considerable skill the twilight zones between the real and the illusionary.

Allied to this existential flexibility – perhaps as an inevitable corollary – is another quality, that of intimacy. Radio whispers in the ear, like a parent telling a bedtime story. We cannot remain distanced from the action, because the action is going on inside our own heads; the slightest sound, the most subtle shift of inflection in a voice, take on a significance impossible in any other medium. When, for instance, we hear Beckett's *All That Fall*, we become a part of the world of Maddy Rooney, a world in which she feels trapped and despairing in her own consciousness. It is an exciting and magical medium – but one in which the Brechtian virtues of objectivity and epic scope seem very hard to achieve. It is all too easy for a political play, with a consistent view of the world and a strong insistence that we pass clear judgement upon a situation, to leave us complaining, like Queen Victoria, that we have been addressed as if we were a public meeting. Radio is above all an experience of individuals.

Arden has succeeded in creating a play about public issues, a play on a large scale, which works perfectly within its medium. In this it is almost unique (perhaps David Rudkin's *Cries from Casement as his Bones are Brought to Dublin*, broadcast in 1973, is its only real equal). He does so by using the intimacy of the microphone to involve us closely in a process of creation. This process is at work from the moment the play begins – a trumpet sounds, we hear the heavy tread of actors booted for tragedy, and they launch into *Julius Caesar*. As the play proceeds, a voice comes close to us; Pearl is speaking – to us or to herself? – about the play, and about her own feelings, for she too is playing a role, she is in disguise as a courtesan and is not happy with the experience. The scene shifts backstage; we are with the actors, talking about the audience, then back to the front of the house – but this time the play is interrupted; a Puritan preacher, Gideon Grip, denounces the players, and in particular the boy-actor, the 'insidious hermaphrodite bramble-bush' playing Calpurnia. In doing so he locates the play for us fairly precisely – it is clearly about 1640 – and also makes it plain that this is an issue of passionate concern. He is engaged almost at once in debate by a man to whom it is equally a matter of life or death, the playwright Tom Backhouse, but this is cut short as the audience catch Grip's fervour and drive the whores from the playhouse. At once, we are back with Pearl, and as we follow her we learn her mission; she is involved in a greater creative process, the making of history.

We hear Pearl in close debate with Tom Backhouse and his patron, Lord Grimscar; the situation they discuss is highly complex and perhaps only the intimacy of the microphone makes it possible to follow its intricacies. The scene is charged with excitement, not through direct action, but through the potential for action which it shows, for these people may be about to change the face of Britain. There is considerable feeling against the King and his Deputy in Ireland, Strafford. Pearl describes the condition of the Irish Catholics, oppressed by the Protestant settlers planted in their lands by the King and on the verge of rebellion. She has come to investigate the possibility of an alliance between the Irish Catholics, the

Scots Presbyterians, already threatened by Strafford's troops, and the English Puritans – in other words, of a People's Revolution, grounded not in religious strife but in solidarity against a common enemy.

Arden thus forces us to reassess whatever pre-conceptions we may have had about this vital period in the history of the two countries; he makes it plain that events as they happened were not inevitable, that there were other possibilities, more fruitful and in some ways more natural. He forces us to look hard at the clichés beloved of the media-men in discussing the present situation – 'sectarian strife', for example. The vision of an alternative history he presents is all the more powerful because we learn about it through Pearl herself. We are close to her; Elizabeth Bell spoke her soliloquies in a special studio with a soft, velvety acoustic so that we seemed to be right inside her head.

Pearl is not really Irish or English. Her Irish mother was sold into slavery as part of Strafford's reprisals for a cattle raid; her father was a Red Indian slaughtered by British colonists. She has wandered over the known world since her twelfth year. Her accent, Irish–Indian overlaid with Spanish and Italian and French and touches from every corner of Europe, is a continuing aural symbol of her status. She speaks for the oppressed in every country who have been driven out by the greed for land which she sees at the root of the Irish troubles. She is thus simultaneously deeply involved in the political issues she narrates and yet apart from them.

To change the course of history is an undertaking so massive the listener can hardly grasp it; Arden renders it apprehensible through a powerful symbol – throughout the whole of *Pearl*, we are involved, as at the beginning, in an intimate creative process, the making of a play. Pearl

149

and Backhouse evolve a plan to write a play which will not only win the English Puritans to the alliance, but which will also win them to the theatre – for, as Backhouse points out, they are the only audience worth the winning:

> – if this stage is from now on capable of holding only the attention of the court-harlots and their embroidered stallions, then Jonson and Shakespeare, Christopher Marlowe and all the rest of 'em might just as well have spent their lives emptying nightsoil into t'village-midden. We spoke once to the whole people. But these days we have rejected the homespun jackets, the square-toed shoes, and the forthright word of the godly tradesmen. And by God they've rejected *us*. There are those in the Parliament have said openly they'd close down every playhouse if they once attained full power. And I *want* them to attain full power. And the whole of my life's work will be broken in two by it . . . .

The play they write is a version of the Esther story – Esther, who brought down Haman, the wicked Deputy of his king. At the end of the play Pearl, playing Esther, intends to step out of her role and appear in Puritan dress to call for the impeachment of Strafford and, if they carry the audience, for that of the King himself. But as rehearsals begin, they find that Grimscar's Royalist mistress has employed a designer-cum-producer, the sinister Captain Catso, and that an alien interpretation is forced upon the play. It begins to centre upon Haman as 'tragic hero', undone by his 'fatal flaw' in the tradition that Brecht hated and which the Puritans will clearly despise. There are titillating costumes and dancing girls, and Pearl finds herself desperately struggling to hide her intentions from Captain Catso and the cast.

At the performance, the Royalist plot is complete. Catso seizes Pearl as she is preparing her transformation scene and forces her to dance naked before the audience; the Puritans are lost for ever, and at that moment we hear the news that the Scots Presbyterians have defeated the King's troops. The English Revolution has begun – but it will be very different from the Revolution that Pearl hoped for.

We have come to share Pearl's aspirations; the idea of social change has become indissolubly linked with the excitement of creation. The play has taken shape as we listened; we have experienced the power which it holds over Backhouse and Pearl; her voice, when she speaks of the theatre, moves effortlessly into verse. She speaks of it in terms of hunger, of lust; she even links it to her own desire for an identity:

Who is the one who is thinking my thoughts,
Who is this woman who turns and turns at the mill of my brain?
And yet how unreasonably exalted would I find myself now had I only been able to see the murder of Julius Caesar right through to the end!

As she and Backhouse work on the Esther play we see a love begin to develop between them. The theatre comes to be seen as a form of nourishment – an image all the more powerful in the mouth of a character who speaks without self-pity of the colossal deprivations she has endured.

Arden ends the play with an alienation effect of shattering force that is peculiarly radiophonic. Pearl has always been close to us; the acoustic ensures that we have the feeling that we share her thoughts. She often acts as a narrator, describing the people and places she sees with great vividness and often in the present tense. Suddenly, as the Royalists sweep backstage, as the Esther play closes in chaos, she switches into a different acoustic, hard and distancing, and narrates as past history an act of extreme violence, the first in the play to touch a character we have come to know. Grimscar's mistress, the thwarted Royalist, snatches Pearl's knife and stabs her: 'She drove the point deep into both of my eyes. And she split my top lip to the division of my nostrils. She cut notches into my cheeks and my ears. After that, they wrapped rags round me: they kicked me out at a back door. . . .'

Pearl has described her body to us; she has been forced throughout the play to change her clothes, her disguise, many times, but the reality of her own skin has remained consistent. Now we have to see her in a new way, and with that knowledge comes the knowledge of the true version of history, the harsh reality of unchanged fact. Arden has used the ability of the medium to create different realities to seduce us into accepting, momentarily, a history that never happened. Now he confronts us with the waste and pain and injustice of the reality:

Civil War came upon England. The King's head was taken off. Civil War came upon Ireland. O'Neill now understood there was not one party in England any good to him any more, and he raised his rebellion as originally intended. He was misleadingly accused of unprecedented bloodshed. As a result, the whole of Ireland was laid waste, oh most barbarous, by the revolutionary army of Oliver Cromwell . . . Every theatre throughout the land was closed down by Act of Parliament: and from that day to this the word of the Common People of England, most powerful in the strength of the Lord, had little or nothing to do with the word of their tragic poets or the high genius of their actors. You might say this did small hurt to the body and bones, but deeper, within the soul. . . . Let them live with it.

We hear Pearl, in a howling wind and crying: 'For the mercy of Christ give a penny to the poor blind woman' as she taps her way into the storm, blind and ugly and dying. The effect is electrifying, rather like the moment in 'St Agnes' Eve' when Keats suddenly distances his warm and living lovers into the 'ages long ago'; but it also makes a sober point – that Pearl, if she ever existed, would be this mutilated outcast, not the living and beautiful figure of our imagination.

The vision of a theatre created in *Pearl* is at once optimistic and terrifyingly pessimistic. It demonstrates the splendour and the dignity possible to a theatre which is created for the people and which has a true political purpose; but it also shows the vulnerability of the writer who attempts to make that creation possible.

Afterword

He thinks, therefore they damn well threw him out.
(John Arden, to Rudi Dutschke)

The experience of theatre which led to my own early interest in Arden was, I imagine, a common one for my generation. As I began reading plays in my teens the serious theatre was clearly shaped by the Big Four: Osborne, Arden, Pinter and Wesker. I say *read* plays, rather than *see* them, because I lived in a provincial town where there were few opportunities for the latter. There was a large and beautiful Victorian theatre, but the plays that appeared there for pre-London tryouts and so on tended to be rather dull thrillers and farces; the most exciting evenings it offered were performances by visiting opera and ballet companies and the odd musical. The only playwright whose work I had much opportunity to see was Shakespeare; and as, at school, he was almost the only playwright studied, and certainly the only playwright we ever performed, it was Shakespeare who really shaped my ideas of what theatre ought to be. I had not much idea of how the work of the Big Four would translate to the stage.

154

Then the Chichester Festival Theatre opened; it was a boldly experimental shape for a playhouse, with a large apron stage like a Jacobean theatre; it worked very well for Jacobean plays, but for modern ones it was rather unsatisfying. Most of them seemed too small for it; the action looked constricted and awkward; one of the few that worked, visually, was Peter Shaffer's play about the Spanish conquest of Peru, *The Royal Hunt of the Sun*; but this wasn't altogether satisfactory either; the language seemed constricted, curiously thin, even though the action filled the stage splendidly.

The only modern plays that really looked as if they were born for the spacious intimacy of Chichester were those of John Arden. *Armstrong's Last Goodnight*, especially, was a revelation to me. The characters did not, as they seemed to in most plays, simply walk on and say their lines or do their business and walk off; they created a whole pattern of energy on the stage so that not a moment was wasted. The dialogue had an amplitude that filled the massive space and which was clearly a joy to speak – the verse in particular seemed to charge the actors with power. It was a phenomenon I had never seen outside the Jacobean drama. Those operas and ballets and musicals, too, had given me a conviction that the theatre should look attractive, that music and colourful costumes were an essential part of a play, but most of the costume plays I had seen seemed rather tacky and trivial. *Armstrong* did not; the visual attractiveness was not just top-dressing, but was there to say something about the world of the play.

I had the opportunity, later, to see other plays in other theatres, but I did not find any reason to change my mind about Arden's status in the theatre; he seemed to be doing more interesting and important work than anyone else. No other playwright seemed to think in these Shakespearean terms, at least not in England. No other playwright seemed to work on the assumption that theatre was such an important medium, that it could and should do things that the novel, or television or film, could never do. The only work in the theatre that held my imagination as Arden's plays had done was the work of the director Peter Brook: his version of the Peter Weiss play, *The Marat/Sade* in 1964, and his production of the Royal Shakespeare Company's collective work on the Vietnam War, *US*, in 1966, had the same massive scope and the same passionate concern with the texture of society.

As I have said, this was probably a common enough experience; my own generation was one of the first to have received the benefits of the Butler Education Act of 1944 and the increased number of university places; it created a large number of people who cared a great deal about theatre, but who had had little access to it – and consequently had very different preconceptions from the critics who attacked Arden for his lack of 'characterization' or his use of verse and song. It created, too, a large number of people who had tried, at least at the school-play level, to create theatre on their own account; drama in schools was increasing all the time.

The rise, then, of so many fringe theatre groups in the late 60s was not surprising; nor was it a coincidence that the best of the writers who came to prominence through these groups – Brenton, for example – were equally capable of working with a small number of actors on a piece of 'rough theatre' at a variety of unorthodox venues, or of thinking in terms of the epic and the Elizabethan. Arden was no longer alone as an exponent of a particular style; he could be judged alongside others in what was coming to be a new tradition.

Within this tradition, perhaps his only equals are Brenton

and Bond. 'We need to set our scenes in public places, where history is formed, classes clash, and whole societies move. Otherwise we're not writing about the events that most affect us and shape out future',[1] wrote Bond in 1978, while the title of Brenton's early collected plays, *Plays for Public Places*[2], anticipates the sort of work he would be doing in the National Theatre in the 70s and 80s, using the stage of the Olivier theatre to create and explore a whole society in, for instance, *The Romans in Britain*.

It would be invidious, not to mention premature, to attempt to place Arden on some sort of twentieth-century league table of the theatre, still less to discuss his place in theatrical history. It seems clear enough, however, that anyone looking at the British theatre of the second half of the twentieth century will find him hard to ignore. It might be prudent to conclude with a look at the factors that may lead to that future 'placing'.

Arden's critics, as I have tried to show, have often called attention to his many virtues while expressing keen dislike of and hostility to the particular play in hand. He is widely acknowledged, however, as a creator of sheer theatrical excitement on a Jacobean scale; his dramatic energy, the frequent beauty of his language, the abundant life of the plays and in particular of figures like Gilnockie and Charlie Butterthwaite are no longer in doubt. In this respect he has been an innovator. If he has not directly influenced Brenton and Bond, he certainly helped to create a context in which their work might be understood. His work with D'Arcy in local communities and with small political groups, too, preceded the upsurge of fringe and community theatre in England. At the very least, it must have given courage to those following after, and, as I have described, in the case of 7.84 it made a real difference to the style in which they chose to work. These activities, too, have quite clearly changed the lives of the people who shared them. Most theatre criticism is still London-based and tends to miss this very obvious fact; but there are people in several walks of life who would now offer a definition of theatre very different from that of, say, a London critic in 1959. The debate as to what theatre is, and for whom, is still going on and Arden is playing an important part.

Arden is also, as I have said, the only major British playwright who has tried consistently over a period of years to present and analyze the relationship between England and Ireland. This fact may, in the end, prove crucial to the establishment of his place in theatre history. His Irish work, with the exception of *Pearl*, has not been well received, and most of the reviews of *Pearl* concentrated upon its treatment of theatricality and its manipulation of levels of reality. There seemed to be no attempts to discuss the political situation it depicted or the implications of that situation for the twentieth century. I have already indicated the level of hostility at which the reviews of Arden's and D'Arcy's other Irish plays were pitched; they were lucky if they were acknowledged as *plays* at all.

Arden lives in Ireland and he is English. He is therefore uniquely qualified to throw light upon a situation that desperately needs it, and he is fully aware of the responsibility this places upon him as a playwright committed to dramatizing society 'to itself and for itself'. Yet the British theatre is, apparently, determined that he shall not discharge that responsibility. The problem is less acute for D'Arcy; as an Irishwoman, she can work in Galway upon home ground, but Arden looks as if he may share O'Casey's fate. O'Casey, his plays rejected in Ireland, worked in England, in exile; and he subsequently found both the matter and the manner of his later political plays attacked or merely dismissed. His reputation has yet to be adequately reassessed; he remains one of the most underestimated writers of his time. Arden has written nothing for the British theatre since 1978, when he collaborated with D'Arcy on *Vandaleur's Folly*. He has, of course, made a fruitful exploration of radio; a new play, *Garland for a Hoar Head*, transmitted, and *Pearl* alone would assure him an honoured place in the history of the medium. But the most recent new Arden work to be heard in England is his radio adaptation of *Don Quixote*. It opens in a prison, where Cervantes is beginning to write, confined in a small cell with an audience of one. If this should turn out to be a symbol or a prophecy of Arden's reception in this country in the next few decades, it will be a tragic and possibly irreparable loss to the theatre.

References

1. Introduction

1. K. Tynan, *Tynan on Theatre* (Penguin, 1964) p. 84.
2. H. Hobson, *Sunday Times*, 25 October 1959.
3. *Punch*, 28 October 1959.
4. K. Stanislavski, *Building a Character*, trans. Hapgood (Eyre Methuen, 1979) pp. 28–9.
5. K. Stanislavski, *On the Art of the Stage*, trans. Magarshack (Faber, 1967) p. 129.
6. R. Williams, *Drama in Performance* (Penguin, 1968) p. 180.
7. B. Brecht, 'A Short Organum for the Theatre', trans. Willett, in *Brecht on Theatre* (Methuen, 1965) p. 204.
8. B. Brecht, 'Theatre for Pleasure or Theatre for Instruction', ibid., p. 71.
9. Ibid., p. 71.
10. *Encore*, 9 October 1965, reprinted from *Peace News*, 30 October 1963.
11. *Daily Mail*, 21 October 1957.
12. *Liverpool Post*, 4 October 1958.
13. R. Hayman, *British Theatre since 1955* (OUP, 1979) pp. 12–13.
14. Ibid., p. 88.
15. R. Hayman, *The Conversion of John Arden* (BBC Radio 3, 1980).

References

2. Resources

1. J. Arden, 'Ancient Principles', *To Present the Pretence* (Eyre Methuen, 1977) p. 12.
2. Ibid., p. 11.
3. J. Arden, *Plays One* (Methuen Master Playwrights, 1977) pp. 5–6.
4. See *Encore*, 11 December 1963.
5. Ibid.
6. *Plays and Players*, January 1972.
7. S. Beckett, *Proust and Three Dialogues* (Calder, 1970) p. 103.
8. See Esslin, *The Peopled Wound* (Methuen, 1970) p. 192n.
9. J. Osborne, *Look Back in Anger* (Faber, 1960) pp. 24–5.
10. B. Brecht. Criticism of the New York Production of *Die Mutter*. trans. Willett, in *Brecht on Theatre* (Methuen, 1965) p. 83.
11. See Tynan, *Tynan Right and Left*, (Longmans, 1967) p. 146.
12. A. Hunt, *Arden* (Eyre Methuen, 1974) p. 119.
13. Prawer, *Marxism and World Literature* (OUP, 1978) p. 214.
14. Note from an essay by R. H. Bowden.
15. Arden, *Plays One* (Methuen Master Playwrights, 1977) p. 8.

3. Manner

1. J. Arden, 'Ben Jonson and the Plumb-line', *To Present the Pretence*, p. 32.
2. K. Tynan, *Observer*, 27 October 1957.
3. S. Beckett, 'The Essential and the Incidental', *Twentieth Century Views*, ed. Kilroy (Spectrum, New Jersey: 1975) p. 167.
4. J. Arden, 'Ecce Hobo Sapiens', ibid., p. 69.
5. Ibid, p. 72.
6. S. O'Casey, 'The Bald Primaqueera', *Blasts and Benedictions*, ed. Ayling (Macmillan, 1967) p. 73.
7. Reprinted as a letter to the *Times*, 20 January 1960.
8. J. Arden, 'Telling a True Tale', *Drama Criticism*, ed. Hinchcliffe, Casebook Series (Macmillan, 1979) p. 213.
9. Ibid., p. 213.
10. J. Osborne, 'The Epistle to the Philistines', *Tribune*, 13 May 1960.
11. Arden, 'Telling a True Tale', p. 214.
12. Ibid., p. 214.
13. J. Holloway, *The Story of the Night* (Routledge, 1961) p. 18.
14. P. Brook, *The Empty Space* (Penguin, 1968) pp. 74–5.

15. *Encore*, September–October 1965.

16. J. Arden, *To Present the Pretence*, p. 156.

17. *Sun*, 4 December 1972.

18. J. Arden, 'Playwrights and Play-Writers', *To Present the Pretence*, p. 177.

4. Matter

1. Quoted Ewen, *Brecht* (Calder and Boyars, 1970) p. 211.

2. J. Whiting, *The Art of the Dramatist*, ed. Hayman (London Magazine Editions, 1970) pp. 152–3.

3. J. R. Taylor, Introduction to *Three Plays*, p. 11.

4. E. Morgan, *Encore*, 7 August 1964.

5. C. Itzin, *Stages in the Revolution* (Eyre Methuen, 1980) p. 29.

6. Quoted P. Roberts, *Bond* (Eyre Methuen, 1980) p. 266.

7. Itzin, *Stages in the Revolution*, p. 31.

8. *New Statesman*, 13 July 1979.

9. Arden, 'What is Theatre For?', *Performance*, September–October 1972.

10. Quoted Itzin, *Stages in the Revolution*, p. 36.

11. S. Craig, *Dreams and Deconstructions* (Amber Lane, 1980) p. 19.

12. 'What is Theatre For?'

13. B. Brecht, 'Theatre for Pleasure or Theatre for Instruction', trans. Willett, in *Brech ton Theatre*, p. 73.

14. J. Arden, M. D'Arcy, 'A Socialist Hero on the Stage', *To Present the Pretence*, p. 96.

15. *Guardian*, quoted in full *Theatre Quarterly* 200, v. (1975–6).

16. Karl Marx, 'The Communist Manifesto', *Essential Works of Marxism* ed. Mendel (Bantam, New York, 1961) p. 13.

17. J. Arden, Epilogue, *To Present the Pretence*, p. 215.

5. 'Serjeant Musgrave's Dance' and 'Ars Longa, Vita Brevis'

1. J. Hainsworth, 'John Arden and the Absurd', *Review of English Literature* vol. 7, 1966, p. 43.

2. P. Day, 'The Early Plays of John Arden', *Modern Drama* vol. 18 (1975) p. 240.

3. J. Arden, 'Telling a True Tale', *Drama Criticism*, ed. Hinchcliffe (Macmillan, 1979) p. 213.

4. A. Kennedy, *Six Dramatists in Search of a Language* (CUP, 1975) p. 222.

References

5. M. O'Connell, 'Ritual Elements in *Serjeant Musgrave's Dance*', *Modern Drama*, February 1971.
6. See *Theatre at Work*, ed. Marowitz/Trussler (Methuen, 1967).
7. A. Brien, *Spectator*, 30 October 1959.
8. Ibid.
9. P. Brook, *The Empty Space* (Penguin, 1968) p. 71.

6. 'The Island of the Mighty' and 'Pearl'

1. D. Jones, *In Parenthesis* (Faber, 1963) p. xiii.
2. David Jones, *Plays and Players*, February 1973. (NB – no relation to the above.)
3. *Guardian*, 6 December 1972.
4. *Tribune*, 15 December 1972.
5. A. Hunt, *Arden* (Eyre Methuen, 1974) postscript.
6. 'The Island of the Ardens', interview with Pam Gems, *Plays and Players*, January 1973.
7. J. Arden, 'The Chhau Dancers of Purulia', *To Present the Pretence*, p. 144.
8. C. Chambers, *Other Spaces* (Eyre Methuen, 1980) p. 15.
9. Robert Graves, *The White Goddess* (Faber, 1961) p. 455.

Afterword

1. E. Bond, 'Us, our Drama and the National Theatre', *Plays and Players*, October 1978.
2. H. Brenton, *Plays for Public Places* (Methuen, 1972).

Chronology of Plays

(First Performance)

All Fall Down   Edinburgh, 1955.

The Life of Man   BBC Radio, 1956.

The Waters of Babylon   London, 1957.

When is a Door not a Door?   London (Central School of Speech and Drama), 1958.

Live Like Pigs   London, 1958.

Serjeant Musgrave's Dance   London, 1959.

Soldier, Soldier   BBC TV, 1960.

The Happy Haven (Arden/D'Arcy)   Bristol, 1960.

The Business of Good Government (Arden/D'Arcy)   Brent Knoll, Somerset, 1960.

Wet Fish   BBC TV, 1961.

The Dying Cowboy   BBC Radio, 1961.

The Workhouse Donkey   Chichester, 1963.

Ironhand   Bristol, 1963.

Ars Longa, Vita Brevis (Arden/D'Arcy) London, 1964

Armstrong's Last Goodnight   Glasgow, 1964.

Left Handed Liberty   London, 1965.

Fidelio (adaptation of a libretto by Sonnleithner and Treitschke)   London, 1965.

Friday's Hiding (Mime, Arden/D'Arcy)   Edinburgh, 1966.

The Royal Pardon (Arden/D'Arcy)   Beaford, Devon, 1966.

The True History of Squire Jonathan and His Unfortunate Treasure   London, 1968.

The Hero Rises Up (Arden/D'Arcy)   London, 1968.

Chronology of Plays

The Soldier's Tale (adaptation of a libretto by Ramuz)   Bath, 1968.

Harold Muggins is a Martyr (Arden, D'Arcy and CAST)   London, 1968.

The Bagman   BBC Radio, 1970.

200 Years of Labour History (D'Arcy, Arden and others, for Socialist Labour League Rally)   London, 1971.

The Ballygombeen Bequest (Arden/D'Arcy)   Belfast, 1972.

The Island of the Mighty (Arden/D'Arcy)   London, 1972.

Keep Those People Moving (D'Arcy/Arden, for children)   BBC Radio, 1972.

Portrait of a Rebel (D'Arcy/Arden)   RTE, 1973.

The Non-Stop Connolly Show (D'Arcy/Arden)   Dublin, 1975.

The Little Gray Home in the West (D'Arcy/Arden)   Sugawn Theatre, 1978.

Vandaleur's Folly (D'Arcy/Arden)   Oxford, 1978.

Pearl   BBC Radio, 1978.

To Put it Frankly . . .   BBC Radio, 1979.

The Menace of Ireland . . . ? (D'Arcy/Arden)   Bradford, 1979.

Don Quixote (2 parts)   BBC Radio, 1980.

Garland for a Hoar Head   BBC Radio, 1982.

165

Bibliography

Where more than one edition is mentioned, that used in the text is named first.

Plays

Three Plays (*The Waters of Babylon*, *Live Like Pigs*, *The Happy Haven*), Arden/D'Arcy (Grove Press, New York: 1961 and Penguin, 1964).

Serjeant Musgrave's Dance (Methuen, 1960 and Grove Press, New York: 1962).

The Business of Good Government, Arden/D'Arcy (Methuen, 1963 and Grove Press, New York: 1967).

The Workhouse Donkey (Methuen, 1964 and Grove Press, New York: 1967).

Armstrong's Last Goodnight (Methuen, 1965 and Grove Press, New York: 1967).

Left Handed Liberty (Methuen, 1965 and Grove Press, New York: 1966).

Ironhand, from Goethe's *Goetz von Berlichingen* (Methuen, 1965).

Soldier, Soldier and Other Plays, including *Wet Fish*, *When is a Door not a Door?* and *Friday's Hiding*, Arden/D'Arcy (Methuen, 1967).

The Royal Pardon, Arden/D'Arcy (Methuen, 1967).

The Hero Rises Up, Arden/D'Arcy (Methuen, 1969).

Two Autobiographical Plays, including *The Bagman* and *The True History of Squire Jonathan and His Unfortunate Treasure* (Methuen, 1971).

Bibliography

The Island of the Mighty, Arden/D'Arcy (Methuen, 1973).

Pearl (Methuen, 1979).

Vandaleur's Folly, D'Arcy/Arden (Methuen, 1981).

Plays One (*Serjeant Musgrave's Dance*, *The Workhouse Donkey*, *Armstrong's Last Goodnight*), Master Playwrights Series (Eyre Methuen, 1977).

Ars Longa, Vita Brevis, Arden/D'Arcy (*Encore*, March 1964 and Cassell, 1965).

The Ballygombeen Bequest, Arden/D'Arcy (Scripts 9, New York: September 1972).

The Non-Stop Connolly Show, 5 vols., D'Arcy/Arden (Pluto Press, 1978).

The Little Gray Home in the West, D'Arcy/Arden (Pluto Press, 1980).

Selected essays by John Arden

To Present the Pretence A collection including two essays written in collaboration with D'Arcy, (Eyre Methuen, 1977).

'Ecce Hobo Sapiens: O'Casey's Theatre, Sean O'Casey' in *Twentieth Century Views*, ed. Kilroy (Spectrum, New Jersey: 1975).

'Telling a True Tale' in *Drama Criticism*, ed. Hinchcliffe, Casebook Series (Macmillan 1979).

Some of John Arden's poetry can be found in *Children of Albion*, ed. Horovitz (Penguin, 1969).

Selected Criticism

Anger and After, J. Russell Taylor, revised edn (Methuen, 1969).

Drama from Ibsen to Brecht, Raymond Williams, revised edn. (Pelican, 1973).

Revolutions in Modern English Drama, Katharine Worth (Bell and Sons, 1972).

Theatre Language, J. Russell Brown (Allen Lane, 1972).

Arden: A Study of his Plays, Albert Hunt (Eyre Methuen, 1974).

Six Dramatists in Search of a Language, A. Kennedy (CUP, 1975).

Anger and Detachment, M. Anderson (Pitman, 1976).

Stages in the Revolution, C. Itzin (Eyre Methuen, 1980).

British Theatre since 1955, R. Hayman (OUP, 1979).

Dreams and Deconstructions, S. Craig (Amber Lane, 1980).

Journals

Two interviews with Walter Wager and Simon Trussler, *Tulane Drama Review*, ii no. 2 (1966).

'Arden's Unsteady Ground', R. Gilman, ibid.

'John Arden and the Public Stage', S. Shrapnel, *Cambridge Quarterly*, IV (Summer 1969).

'John Arden and the Absurd', J. Hainsworth, *Review of English Literature*, vol. 7 no. 4, October 1966.

'Ritual Elements in *Serjeant Musgrave's Dance*', M. O'Connell, *Modern Drama*, February 1971.

Index

Index

Index

Index

Index